Blue Collar Devotions

David Love

A collection of "Pastor's Pen" devotionals written while planting a church in a coastal community.

© Copyright 2005 David Love.
All rights reserved. No part of this publication may be reproduced, stored in a retrieval system, or transmitted, in any form or by any means, electronic, mechanical, photocopying, recording, or otherwise, without the written prior permission of the author.

Note for Librarians: A cataloguing record for this book is available from Library and Archives Canada at www.collectionscanada.ca/amicus/index-e.html
ISBN 1-4120-6531-3

Printed in Victoria, BC, Canada. Printed on paper with minimum 30% recycled fibre. Trafford's print shop runs on "green energy" from solar, wind and other environmentally-friendly power sources.

TRAFFORD
PUBLISHING

Offices in Canada, USA, Ireland and UK

This book was published *on-demand* in cooperation with Trafford Publishing. On-demand publishing is a unique process and service of making a book available for retail sale to the public taking advantage of on-demand manufacturing and Internet marketing. On-demand publishing includes promotions, retail sales, manufacturing, order fulfilment, accounting and collecting royalties on behalf of the author.

Book sales for North America and international:
Trafford Publishing, 6E–2333 Government St.,
Victoria, BC v8t 4p4 CANADA
phone 250 383 6864 (toll-free 1 888 232 4444)
fax 250 383 6804; email to orders@trafford.com

Book sales in Europe:
Trafford Publishing (UK) Limited, 9 Park End Street, 2nd Floor
Oxford, UK ox1 1hh UNITED KINGDOM
phone 44 (0)1865 722 113 (local rate 0845 230 9601)
facsimile 44 (0)1865 722 868; info.uk@trafford.com

Order online at:
trafford.com/05-1442

10 9 8 7 6 5 4 3 2 1

Dedicated to ...

To my fantastic wife, Martha,
my wonderful and gifted kids and their spouses;
Tony and Irene Love, Susan and Mat Bartee with
Alex, Aaron, Adam & Andrew.
I am ever grateful for their support and love.

To Jesus Christ...
The entire reason this whole experience happened.
May He be pleased and glorified.
I'm soooo grateful for His support and love !

Scripture references are from New American Standard Bible

Introduction ... or ... What This Book Is About

"Blue Collar Devotional"? What a strange name! For the most part, this collection of thoughts is the result of eight years of pioneering and pastoring a fledgling church in Anacortes, Washington. When my wife and indispensable helpmate, Martha, and I moved to Anacortes in October of 1983, it was in obedience to a call of God to reach people for Christ through the planting of a Foursquare church. What an experience!

The preceding two decades of my life earning a living had been devoted to the auto-body trade. Knowing what it is to work long hours in a noisy, dirty environment to earn a paycheck, I understand what it is to be "Blue Collar". As we began to see the Lord bring the new church to life, I was aware my perspective was definitely colored by who I was, a Body-man learning to become a Pastor. Committing ourselves to the task, it was necessary for us to have employment to provide income, so Martha worked in Dietary at the local hospital, and I at an auto-body repair shop. Both of us functioned in the Blue Collar world. This brief explanation brings me to the "Why" of this publication.

Early in my pioneering endeavor, I found it necessary to develop various means of communicating with the people whom the Lord was bringing into our fellowship. My days were taken by the demands of the body-shop, so I found I needed to devote early morning and evening hours to study, writing, being with family, responding to needs of the congregation, etc.. There never seemed to be adequate opportunity to share my heart, so I began to write a short, devotional type of article for our weekly bulletin, a "Pastor's Pen", wherein I was able to share various thoughts, concerns, exhortations, encouragement, and news to our congregation. As the years slipped by, the stack of bulletins on my shelf continued to grow until they numbered nearly four hundred.

Following the "passing of the baton" to a new Pastor for our church, I was sifting through the collection of devotionals and the desire to compile some of them into a book format began to somehow become important, so I tried to sort out those I felt would be timeless and generally applicable. This endeavor produced the excerpts you hold in your hand.

This book is probably unlike others you've seen because my purpose was to provide a devotional sans what I call the "Inherent Guilt Factor". My observation has been that most devotionals are arranged very systematically, i.e., a reading for each day or week or month or millennia ... or something. I find I don't respond well to these because I can't seem to maintain the author's timeline. Face it, there are those of us like that, right? If you find yourself in that camp, this collection is for you. I wanted a book I could open to any page and read something brief that could perhaps make my day a little easier to deal with ... are you like that? Some of these are quite brief, some longer, none more than a page or so in length, so they all read quickly.

Not all this material is original with me, but it's all shared with a pure motive ... to point folks to a personal relationship with Christ. However, one act of organization to which I have submitted is to place those articles regarding Christmas and Easter in separate sections.

The sole purpose of it all is for Jesus to be glorified, and your life in Him to be enriched.

May it be.

        Because of Jesus ....
                Dave Love

Christmas

"Unto Us a Child is Born"

IT'S ADVENT SEASON

AND BEHOLD, YOU WILL CONCEIVE IN YOUR WOMB, AND BEAR A SON, AND YOU SHALL NAME HIM JESUS
(Luke 1:31)

So unfolds the miracles of miracles. The virgin maid, Mary, was chosen by our Father to birth His only begotten Son into this world. *"You shall name Him Jesus"* carried knowledge and revelation for those in that time which we would probably miss. They would understand the name "Jesus" was the same as the Old Testament "Yeshua", or, "Joshua", meaning, "The Lord is salvation".

Advent season covers the four Sundays before Christmas, preparing us for the celebration of His first coming --- His Advent. "Advent" means, "to come", and Christmas is the observance of His first Advent. Rejoicing in His first coming should then redirect our focus on what will be His Second Advent, for Jesus our Lord is coming again! He will come this time, not as a new-born infant, but as King of Kings!

Entering the Christmas season, let me suggest two things that can allow the season to be a blessing ---

1. In all your preparations, keep Jesus Christ as the focal point of everything.
2. Resist the "peer pressure" of traditional commercialism to drive you into debt.

I say this because I know the temptation is great to succumb to high powered advertising and offers of easy credit. Christmas is a time for Jesus. Gift giving is fun, and nice, but let it be from His provision and blessing, not from falling into bondage to a plastic card. Being careful in December allows January to be a pleasant month.

May God grant us His wisdom and confidence to live for Him, and may we draw closer to Jesus in this interval of Advent.

BE COMFORTED

THEN THE GLORY OF THE LORD WILL BE REVEALED, AND ALL FLESH WILL SEE IT TOGETHER; FOR THE MOUTH OF THE LORD HAS SPOKEN IT

(Isaiah 40:5)

This season is made even more glorious by the magnificent music of Handel's "Messiah". The above verse is included in one section covering Isaiah 40:1-5, beginning with, *"Comfort, comfort ye My people ..."*. These five verses contain ....

> Prophecy of peace and forgiveness of sin
> Preparation for Messiah by John the Baptist
> The birth of Jesus and His second coming

Quite a lot for five verses, isn't it? I hope you will read it all. But, what does this have to do with Christmas? It has everything to do with it, because it points to the One who was to be born in a stable, the One who was to go to the Cross for our sin, the One who will return again for His Bride, the Church.

We have a glorious future and hope, if we receive Jesus Christ as Savior and Lord of our lives. I have thought, *"If I could give all the people in this church a gift, what would be the very best for them?"* Well, I don't play the Lottery, so no chance for you in that. I'm not much of a cook, so a gourmet dinner wouldn't do it. I don't have a new car to give you (besides, the Lord seems to use the old ones to help us grow, doesn't He?) Let's see, what can I give?

All I can give you is the message of the Gospel, and my love. I can assure you all the promises of the Bible are for you. I can tell you God loved you so much He sent Jesus, His Son, into this stained world so you, personally, can have a hope for the future, a glorious hope. I can tell you He inspired Isaiah to pen those words in Isaiah 40 for you ... today.

I take it personally and seriously when He said, *"Comfort, comfort My people."*

Receive His comfort, He loves you!

YIELDING TO THE NEW BIRTH

AND THE ANGEL ANSWERED AND SAID TO HER, "THE HOLY SPIRIT WILL COME UPON YOU AND THE POWER OF THE MOST HIGH WILL OVERSHADOW YOU; AND FOR THAT REASON THE HOLY OFFSPRING SHALL BE CALLED THE SON OF GOD"
(Luke 1:35)

Jesus Christ was born <u>into</u> this world, not <u>from</u> it. He was not a person that evolved out of history, He came into history from the outside. He was not a man becoming God, but God becoming man, coming in human flesh from the "outside". His life is the highest and holiest, entering in at the lowest of doors. Just as He came into history from the outside, He must come to us from the outside.

We must allow our personal, human life to become a "Bethlehem" for the Son of God. We must have a new birth within. It's a foundational fact the entrance to His Kingdom is through being born from above. The main characteristic of the new birth is that we yield completely to God so that Christ may be formed in us ... and His nature <u>can</u> work through us. As we observe His birth into the world, be reminded of His birth in your heart, and the results following such a step of faith.

Glory to God indeed! *"...The holy offspring shall be called the Son of God".*

CHRISTMAS IS A MIRACLE!

THEREFORE, THE LORD HIMSELF WILL GIVE YOU A SIGN; BEHOLD, A VIRGIN SHALL BE WITH CHILD AND BEAR A SON, AND SHE WILL CALL HIS NAME EMMANUEL (Isaiah 7:14)

At Ahaz's refusal to ask God for a sign, God laid out this promise of a miracle, not just to Ahaz, but to the whole house or linage of David. God would choose a virgin to conceive and bear a son ... He would *be "God with us"*, a Divine Son from the line of David.

Anyone who says the virgin birth of Jesus isn't true or important, is probably anti-supernatural and wants to deny, or give a natural explanation for miracles. What a difficult position that is to maintain! I recently read that even if by some freak accident a virgin did give birth, it would be a girl, for the mother's body cannot produce the chromosomes necessary for a boy. The virgin birth had to involve a miracle whereby God, through His Holy Spirit, created what was necessary for a boy ... The Boy ... would be born.

As we move into the Christmas season, it's good to be mindful of the wonderful miracles forming the very foundation of the eternal life we have been offered. The life of Jesus, from birth to the cross and beyond, abounds with miracles. What miracle do you need? Do you believe the God who caused a virgin to conceive and bear the Son of God can provide the miracle you need?

This is where you say, "YES! HALLELUJAH!"

"I BRING YOU GOOD NEWS OF A GREAT JOY ..."

The second chapter of Luke contains the most complete account of the birth of Jesus. The key verses of this chapter would be 10 & 11, which tell us ...

"AND THE ANGEL SAID TO THEM, 'DO NOT BE AFRAID, FOR BEHOLD, I SHALL BRING YOU GOOD NEWS OF A GREAT JOY WHICH SHALL BE FOR ALL PEOPLE; FOR TODAY IN THE CITY OF DAVID THERE HAS BEEN BORN FOR YOU A SAVIOR, WHICH IS CHRIST THE LORD'"

Note the specific things mentioned that are for us:

1. Don't be afraid.
2. The news is GOOD!
3. It's for ALL!
4. The Savior was born for YOU!
5. He is Christ, the Anointed One.
6. He is Lord, Master of all that is, was, and ever will be!

I've found it interesting, and unusual, that the angels appeared to "some shepherds". Not in the Town Square, not from the peak of Mt. Everest, not downtown Jerusalem, Chicago, or Seattle, but simply to "some shepherds".

The announcement of the coming of God in the flesh, The Great Shepherd, came to those who understood the meaning of being a shepherd. What does it mean to be a shepherd? We all probably have some idea, but the bottom line is that he is a servant, one who gives his life for the care of the flock. We all have people God has placed in our lives so we might be a shepherd to them. As we dutifully care for these, we can expect to know His presence and can sing with the angels, *"Glory to God in the highest ... for today in the city of David there has been born for YOU a Savior who is Christ the Lord!"*

May the Peace, Joy, and Expectation of Christmas fill your life, overflowing with His Holy Spirit!

You are loved!

THE INCREASE OF HIS GOVERNMENT

FOR A CHILD WILL BORN TO US, A SON WILL BE GIVEN TO US; AND THE GOVERNMENT WILL REST UPON HIS SHOULDERS; AND HIS NAME SHALL BE CALLED WONDERFUL, COUNSELOR, MIGHTY GOD, ETERNAL FATHER, PRINCE OF PEACE
(Isaiah 9:6)
THERE WILL BE NO END TO THE INCREASE OF HIS GOVERNMENT OR OF PEACE, ON THE THRONE OF DAVID, AND OVER HIS KINGDOM, TO ESTABLISH IT AND UPHOLD IT WITH JUSTICE AND RIGHTEOUSNESS FROM THEN ON AND FOREVERMORE. THE ZEAL OF THE LORD OF HOSTS WILL ACCOMPLISH THIS
(Isaiah 9:7)

We so often use Isaiah 9:6 in our Christmas devotions, but little is said about verse seven. It seems our generation is one of political turmoil of one kind or another; assassinations, Watergate, foreign aid controversy, terrorism, graft in various administrations, etc.

As we rejoice in the prophecy of verse six, proclaiming the fullness of the Savior, we should just as surely rejoice in the promise of verse seven, i.e., *"There will be no end to the increase of His government or of peace."*

God is establishing His rule in this perverted world. All the while Satan is brewing trouble and making loud noises, drawing our attention to his antics, God is laying the foundation of His government...Eternal Reign! His administration is about to take office! Hallelujah! You can be assured our Party wins!

Through the Christmas season, don't allow the turmoil of the world crowd out the still, small voice of His Spirit. Be at peace, for, *"There will be no end to the increase of His government."*

He loves you!!!

FOR UNTO US

If I were to be put on the spot about a favorite verse concerning the birth of Christ, Isaiah 9:6 would surely be a contender.

FOR UNTO US A CHILD IS BORN, UNTO US A SON IS GIVEN, AND THE GOVERNMENT WILL BE UPON HIS SHOULDERS, AND HIS NAME SHALL BE CALLED WONDERFUL COUNSELOR, MIGHTY GOD, EVERLASTING FATHER, PRINCE OF PEACE.

- Wonderful Counselor: "Wonderful", in this context, refers to being supernatural. The Messiah who came to bring us eternal life. When He comes again, He will rule with perfect wisdom. We can fully expect Him to be a supernatural Counselor for us as we call on His name.
- Mighty God: This is a term referring to YAHWEH, the Almighty God who has ultimate victory over the evil one through Jesus Christ, Messiah. This is the God in whom nothing is too difficult.
- Eternal Father: Literally means, "Father of Eternity". Messiah is forever! A Father to His people, guarding, supplying, and caring for their needs.
- Prince of Peace: He is the One who brings peace in the fullest sense of wholeness, prosperity, and tranquility. We can know His peace now, and eternally.

These insights to Isaiah 9:6 are highly significant, and quite true. However, until you and I receive Jesus as Lord, they only remain words on a page.

In this season of joy, I encourage you to give some thought to this --- are you allowing God to be God in all His facets? Is He the One you look to for counsel? Is He the One you accept as all powerful, able, and willing, to do the impossible for you, and with you? Is He the One who is forever, and because He lives, you may live also? Is He the One who is your peace, your place of refuge, the One to whom you turn in your darkest hour ... and in your greatest joy, as well?

"Jesus, come in Your strength and Your power and Your counsel and Your peace ... be King in our lives!"

LIFE WAS REAL FOR MARY AND JOSEPH

AND IT CAME ABOUT THAT WHILE THEY WERE THERE, THE DAYS WERE COMPLETED FOR HER TO GIVE BIRTH. AND SHE GAVE BIRTH TO HER FIRST BORN SON; AND SHE WRAPPED HIM IN CLOTHES AND LAID HIM IN A MANGER, BECAUSE THERE WAS NO ROOM FOR THEM IN THE INN (Luke 2:6-7)

As we read this part of what we call, "The Christmas Story", I have the distinct feeling I'm not quite able to relate to it. Oh, I can read it, and even understand the experience of the moment. Mary was having a baby in barn, a very unsanitary place, at best. In spite of the fact she knew this baby was special, it was still to be a birth ... with all that implies. Every mother can relate to this, I'm sure.

Joseph would be concerned, even worried, perhaps. He might be frustrated and frightened, because he knew he couldn't provide better for Mary, in spite of his efforts. It was a holy time. It was an event destined to alter the course of history.

This lonely experience of Joseph and Mary would impact the whole world! Did they know that? Probably not. Did they fully understand the significance of the trial they were experiencing? I doubt it. I do believe they were assured of God's presence, and that they probably knew more than we give them credit for.

Mary had been visited by an angel, she knew she had conceived a child by the Holy Spirit. Joseph had also been assured this was indeed true. There should be no question they had placed their trust in God, and knew He would be faithful to bring them through this time of their life.

Joseph and Mary were people. Yes, God had chosen them for a very unique assignment, just as He had others in the past, and still does today ... but, they were still people, like us. They knew pain and fear and discouragement. They also knew peace and laughter and courage ... they knew God.

Christmas season is a good time to be reminded God used what He wanted to use to accomplish what He desired. The Bible says they, *"Found favor with God"*. That says volumes about their relationship with the Lord.

When you find yourself facing inevitable difficulty, think of Joseph and Mary in the barn. The Lord of Hosts surrounded them ... as He will you.

ADVENT

"HAIL, FAVORED ONE! DO NOT BE AFRAID, MARY, FOR YOU HAVE FOUND FAVOR WITH GOD. AND BEHOLD, YOU WILL CONCEIVE IN YOUR WOMB AND BEAR A SON, AND YOU SHALL NAME HIM JESUS"
(Luke 1:28,30-31)

Speaking these words to Mary, the angel Gabriel signaled the unfolding of the first advent of our Lord Jesus.

"Advent", means, "to come". Advent season is the four weeks before Christmas wherein we prepare for the celebration of the birth of the Christ Child. It is a wonderful time. As our thoughts are directed toward this
pivotal point of history, we are reminded that our Savior has come!

It would be well to guard our priorities as the season progresses. It's not always easy to resist the commercial pressures of the world as Christmas draws near. We will be confronted with Santa Claus, Rudolph, Jingle bells, etc., as the world of commerce competes for our dollars. However, I encourage you to be especially sensitive to the purpose of our celebration ... the birth, the Advent, of our Lord and Savior, Jesus Christ.

As the events of the miraculous birth happened in the humble stable, I seriously doubt anyone was thinking about Hallmark, J.C. Penney's, or Walmart. Can you hear Joseph musing to himself, "Let's see now, how can Mary and I market this event? I wonder if Hallmark would be interested in a series of cards about it?" Hmmmmm. Now, I'm not a "Scrooge", saying it's wrong to exchange gifts or have a Christmas tree ... quite the contrary. There are many wonderful Christmas traditions to be enjoyed, but entering this season together, I encourage you to pray about your priorities. It is to be a time of peace, a time of praise and joy, a time to give thanks, to give love, and a time to give yourself to God.

Expect His Advent!

A NEW WAY

"SINCE THEREFORE, BRETHREN, WE HAVE CONFIDENCE TO ENTER THE HOLY PLACE BY THE BLOOD OF JESUS, BY A NEW A LIVING WAY WHICH HE INAUGURATED FOR US THROUGH THE VEIL, THAT IS, HIS FLESH, AND SINCE WE HAVE A GREAT PRIEST OVER THE HOUSE OF GOD, LET US DRAW NEAR, WITH A SINCERE HEART IN FULL ASSURANCE OF FAITH ..." (Hebrews 10:19-22a)

Strange Scripture to use for Christmas? Ah, but you see, the "New and living way" was becoming apparent, visual even, as the birth of the Messiah, the Christ-child, was happening.

When God came to Earth in the form of a tiny baby, He was about to complete another phase of His plan of Redemption ... the ability of sinful man to draw near to a sinless God, through the shed blood of the Son. The tiny baby was to be the sacrifice, once for all. God had made a new way! He has made many "new ways". The wise men were warned by God to return a different way, a "new way", otherwise, their lives would be in danger. God told Joseph to get the Child out of Bethlehem ..."Go all the way to Egypt, and stay there until Herod is dead", he was told. This was a "new way", not the way to Jerusalem.

How do suppose Mary and Joseph afforded the trip? Were the gifts brought by the Wise Men God's provision for such a journey and exile? We're not told that, however, God knew what He was doing. He's quite a practical God, you know. Another "new way"? Perhaps.   Following the death of Herod, God directed Joseph to take the Child and His mother back to Israel. As he was headed for Jerusalem, he was re-routed once again, settling in Nazareth. He was led another "new way". You can read all this in Matthew 2:1-23.

What is your need this Christmas? As the world spins toward the Second Coming of the King (Hallelujah!), needs seem to grow more intense. They are things that cannot be satisfied with a few gifts under a tree, regardless of beauty or cost. It is vital we turn to the One who can meet every need ... Jesus. He is The Way ... The Only Way. This Christmas, remember, God loves you, and He has made a New and Living Way! Let us draw near. Merry Christmas! You are loved!

WHADJAGIT?

Recalling the Christmas' when I a was young, swingin' bachelor of seven or eight, there seemed to be an unspoken law that emerged each Christmas Day. The kids in the neighborhood would gravitate toward one another as soon as possible following the opening of the gifts. Of course, there would always be one guy who got to open everything on Christmas Eve. Poor guy, he never really seemed to fit in. He never knew what it was to experience the excitement and trauma of having to endure "The Night Before". You know, the time when imaginations run wild in anticipation of what the morning would bring. (I wonder what ever happened to him? Probably still opening presents Christmas Eve.) Anyway, as we congregated, there was a word spoken that was common to those skilled in speaking "Kidese". (You know, like Japanese, Chinese ... Kidese) The word was "Whadjagit?" Now, a little research here will reveal this is a "Kidese" contraction of the phrase, "What did you get?" This was a very important event in our young lives. Even though we didn't realize it then, we were forming values. What we received as a gift from one who loved us, became a yardstick of where we fit in our peer group. (It used to just be "other kids", now it's a "peer group") Some things were expensive, some were not, that didn't seem to matter so much. The main thing was, did it make others envious? Was it something that made the proud, new owner "stand out" and be considered real "lucky". Many of us learned our social skills and how to live in this world through experiences such as this, and countless others, just as shallow and distorted.

I've often thought how wonderful it would have been if that bunch of kids, including me, could have had someone instill Godly teaching into our little sinful hearts. I'm sure life would have been much easier to bear. Christmas mornings would have been a time of joy, instead of potential disappointment.

What a contrast Christmas is now! I would love to relive one of those "Whadjagit" times with the other kids. As I would come running from my house to the prearranged gathering spot, the question would meet me before I could catch my breath..."Hey, Dave! Whadjagit?" I can just see the look on their faces as I would loudly and joyfully proclaim ... **"I GOT JESUS!!! WHADJOOGIT?"''**

For where your treasure is, there will be your heart also". (Matt.6:21)

By the way ... Whadjagit?

IT'S A MIRACULOUS SEASON

FOR NOTHING WILL BE IMPOSSIBLE FOR THE LORD
(Lk.1:37)

That's what it says, "NOTHING"! A pretty strong statement, isn't it? For me, this verse stands out as beacon in the account of the First Advent, that portion of the Bible we call "The Christmas Story".

The events unfolding were totally miraculous, as Father God brought His plan of Redemption into being. Zachariah's experience in the Temple was a miracle. The conception and birth of Jesus was a miracle. The safety, growth, and ministry of the One born in a stable was a miracle. The prophesied Crucifixion of God's Son was a miracle. His triumphant Resurrection was a miracle. The love He pours out for us is a miracle. His healing in our bodies, minds, and spirits is a miracle. Do you believe in miracles? The fact you are alive and able to read this is a miracle. You are not a product of evolution, emanating from a blob of slime. (Yuk!) You are a product of God's own hand, lovingly created for fellowship with Him. (Hallelujah!) You are loved by Him, and, believing on Jesus, will spend eternity with Him.

The individual events of the birth of Christ are truly astounding and marvelous, and through it all, I'm constantly amazed at the God of the impossible. He makes possible that which could never be accomplished any other way. Christmas season is to be a time of joy, regardless of circumstances. It's not dependent on gifts, glitz, or hype. It's dependent on a relationship with the miracle working King of all kings, Lord of all lords.

This season is a good time to present ourselves anew to the Babe who became the Resurrected One, and is coming again very soon. He is abounding in miracles, for ... WITH GOD, NOTHING IS IMPOSSIBLE!

Can you say, "Amen"?

O COME LET US ADORE HIM

AND THE ANGEL SAID TO THEM, DO NOT BE AFRAID, FOR BEHOLD, I BRING YOU GOOD NEWS OF A GREAT JOY WHICH SHALL BE FOR ALL THE PEOPLE
(Luke 2:10)

What a night that must have been for the shepherds! There they were, minding their own business tending the flock. They were simply "standing watch". From the military perspective, they were on "guard duty". A person on guard duty may not do much physically, but they are to observe, be watchful, and if anything strange happens, they are to take appropriate action.

As watchful as the shepherds may have been that night, they were probably not prepared for what happened. As Luke 2:9 says, *"An angel of the Lord SUDDENLY stood before them and the glory of the Lord shone around them, and they were terribly frightened."* The Greek here indicates it happened in a flash. "Suddenly", means just that ... ZAP!

Looking back from our perspective, we may think those shepherds weren't very spiritual. If they were "tuned in" to the Lord, they would have expected this and their reaction would have been different. Some may think they would politely say, *"How wonderful for you to come, Angel. What a blessing it is for you to grace our lives with this display of your heavenly presence, etc., etc.."* Fat chance! If we were there, our reaction would have been the same as theirs ... *"Yikes! What's going on? Hit the deck, we're under attack! Help! God! Are You out there? Help us!"* Get the idea?

This portion of the Christmas story expands my understanding of God. What seems to be the hum-drum of life (Believe me, guard duty can be very hum-drum) can often be the setting God uses to come crashing into our life in an unexpected fashion. That's when it usually happens to me. He doesn't do it to cause fear, but blessing and good news. The initial reaction of the angel was to calm them and dispel fear. What are we to do? Keep watching, our turn is coming. *"Behold, I tell you a mystery, we shall not all sleep, but we shall all be changed in a moment, in the twinkling of an eye..."* (1 Cor15:51-52a)

Watch ... and expect!

TREASURING ... AND PONDERING

"Can this really be happening to me?" This surely must have been among the thoughts passing through Mary's mind as she and Joseph found themselves in a strange manger with a newborn son.

Miraculously, many people found their way to them. Shepherds came with startling accounts of an angel who had appeared to them, proclaiming the uniqueness of this infant ... He is the Savior! What was Mary to do with that information? How would you feel? What would you think? Luke 2:19, tells us, *"Mary treasured up all these things, pondering them in her heart."* She had received a promise from God. It was delivered by men who were probably still grubby from the field and their travel, but it was from the Lord. None of her circumstances seemed religious or holy, yet, she had a promise! And ... she "treasured it up".

Mary has provided a good example for us. We too, should "treasure up and ponder". Do you ever ponder the things of God? Pondering is deep thinking, a careful consideration of something. Do you ponder your salvation? Think of it! God has forgiven you of your sin! He has made a way for you to be with Him forever! How about the time He healed you? Or when He kept your children from harm. Or when He provided financially. Or when He brought that special person into your life. Or just the time when He made His presence known, and you felt His love for you.

There are numerous things to think of that may invoke fear or depression. Who needs it? Do you think Mary was thrilled with her birthing room decorated in "Early Stable" motif? Not likely. But she heard the wondrous news, and she treasured it up and pondered it in her heart. What has God been doing in your life? Paul says, *"Let your mind dwell on these things."* (Philippians 4:8)

Try it ... You'll like it!

Easter

He is Risen!

TIME FOR CELEBRATION

AND AS HE WAS APPROACHING, NEAR THE DESCENT OF THE MOUNT OF OLIVES, THE WHOLE MULTITUDE OF THE DISCIPLES BEGAN TO PRAISE GOD JOYFULLY WITH A LOUD VOICE FOR ALL THE MIRACLES THEY HAD SEEN, SAYING, "BLESSED IS HE WHO COMES IN THE NAME OF THE LORD; PEACE IN HEAVEN AND GLORY IN THE HIGHEST.
(Luke 19:37-38)

Jesus descended from Mt. Olive into the midst of noise and activity, there surely must have been some intense feelings in the air! The whole scene is one of pandemonium, yet, the Messiah maintained His bearing and authority. There was great excitement; there were people for Him, and those who opposed Him. The entry of Jesus into Jerusalem was a time of great celebration ... if you were a Believer. If you were a Pharisee, it was a time of trouble. The Pharisees told Jesus to make His disciples be quiet, to quit giving Him glory. His reply was, *"I tell you, if these become silent, the stones will cry out!"* When it's time for celebration in the Kingdom ... there is celebration!

The same holds true for us today! Because Jesus entered Jerusalem, because He was crucified, because He was buried, because He burst forth from the tomb, we have great cause for celebration! God is to be worshipped. If His people are silenced, all creation will bow down and worship, giving Him praise.

None of us were there that day as this phenomenal event unfolded, but we can still give Him glory and honor and praise ... just as they did then.

Blessed is the King who comes in the name of the Lord!

HE DID IT FOR YOU

AND JESUS, CRYING OUT WITH A LOUD VOICE, SAID, "FATHER, INTO THY HANDS I COMMIT MY SPIRIT"; AND HAVING SAID THIS, HE BREATHED HIS LAST
(Luke 23:46)

AND JESUS CRIED OUT AGAIN WITH A LOUD VOICE, AND YIELDED UP HIS SPIRIT
(Matt.27:50)

AND JESUS UTTERED A LOUD CRY, AND BREATHED HIS LAST
(Mark 15:37)
AND HE BOWED HIS HEAD AND GAVE UP HIS SPIRIT
(John 19:30b)

The death of Jesus, a black day for sure. Today we call it "Good Friday", which may not seem to make sense. However, Sunday's coming! I think we are well acquainted with the miracle that happened the day the tomb was found empty ... Jesus was risen from the dead! What a miracle! But you know, Friday was a miracle, too. We must remember no man in all history ever had the power to dismiss His spirit by his own choice and will. Jesus miraculously handed over His spirit to the Father when He had paid the price for our sin. He had power available to do whatever He pleased.
John 10:18, tells us ...

NO MAN HAS TAKEN MY LIFE FROM ME, I LAY IT DOWN ON MY OWN INITIATIVE. I HAVE AUTHORITY TO TAKE IT UP AGAIN. THIS COMMANDMENT I RECEIVED FROM MY FATHER.

There was a miracle at Calvary on Friday, as well as a miracle in the tomb on Easter morning.
Think of it ... He did it for you!

LENT

Lent is a time of preparation for the celebration of Easter. It is a period of fasting and "heart preparation". Another benefit is that "Lent" originally meant "Spring", that special time of year when new beginnings are stirring.

Perhaps this Lenten season will bring new beginnings for you. In a courtroom, if someone states something the jury isn't supposed to hear, the judge will say, "Strike that from the record." The stenographer wouldn't be allowed to put it into the court proceedings, so when the final draft of the trial was written, there would be no record of it.

When we come to the Lord and ask forgiveness of our sins, He says, "Strike that from the record." It is gone ... it doesn't exist any longer! There is no reason for you to feel guilt ... there is no record of your sin.

Sometimes, I think we need a "starting point" for a change. If you are feeling that need, perhaps this is a good spot to begin ... Lent. It's a time of preparation leading to Easter ...the ultimate victory of Christ over the powers of darkness.

A new beginning indeed! As the Apostle Paul said, *"Forgetting what lies behind, and reaching forward to lies ahead, I press on ... "* (Philippians 3:13-14)

Jesus loves you!

EXPECTANCY!

HOSANNA TO THE SON OF DAVID; BLESSED IS HE WHO COMES IN THE NAME OF THE LORD; HOSANNA IN THE HIGHEST!
(Matthew 21:9)

This acclamation of the people of Jerusalem is based on the words of Psalm 118:25-27. This is the event we celebrate as we observe "Palm Sunday". This historic event points me toward a word God is confronting us with lately ... EXPECTANCY!

There was certainly an atmosphere of expectancy that day as Jesus rode into town on that donkey! People were expecting to be released from the oppression of Roman rule, but little did they expect the spiritual salvation unfolding before them. The disciples, and all those who were followers of Jesus, were surely anticipating something to take place, though they weren't sure just what it would be.

Jesus, Himself, was moving in great expectancy. He was anticipating the most world-changing week in all history. He was expecting to be faithful to the Father's will; He was expecting the suffering and torment from the Roman soldiers, the brokenness of His body, and the indescribable event of the Crucifixion. But ...BUT ... He was also expecting triumph! Victory over all the power of Satan was about to be established, guaranteed for all time!

It is wise for us to expect also. More than wise, it is imperative! We should gather for worship with expectancy pulsating in every fiber of our being! We can live daily, in all of life's experiences, with a sense of expectancy; listening, anticipating, expecting God!

During this marvelous Easter season, expect the Resurrected Christ to effect change in your life, change
that will draw you closer to Jesus than ever ... and to each other.
EXPECT!

EASTER ... EGG HUNTS OR AN EMPTY GRAVE?

I look forward to seeing newspaper ads about various Easter services to be held. The one speaking most pointedly to me this year was the ad from the Lutheran Church. Displaying an artist's concept of Jesus, it read, *"HE DIDN'T RISE FROM THE DEAD TO HUNT EASTER EGGS."*

Now, any upright, card-carrying Christian would say, "Well, of course not, that's silly!" Tragically, a lot of people don't know there is more to Easter than a rabbit that has somehow mastered the art of laying colored eggs. Easter is no mystery to those willing to do even a slight amount of research.

"Easter" is the English rendition of "Pascha", the Greek word for Passover. For example, the King James Version uses the word "Easter" in Acts 12:4, concerning Peter's arrest. Other versions have changed it to "Passover", for that is what it is.

There was a difference of opinion in the early church about when to celebrate the Resurrection. The Jewish Christians linked it to Passover, regardless of the day of the week. The Gentile believers observed it on Sunday. This problem was finally solved at the Council of Nicea in 325 A.D.. They ruled it would be celebrated on the first Sunday after the full moon following the vernal equinox (when the sun crosses the equator in the spring).

That's why Easter falls on so many different Sundays. This year (1989) is one of the earliest occurrences, and it can be as late as April 25th. However, even trying to understand the proper day can obscure the focal point of the whole event.

Jesus Christ was crucified, was dead, was buried, and on the third day He rose again! He rose again! He rose again! HE ROSE AGAIN! Now, that's the REAL story of Easter!

May His resurrection be yours also!

HOSANNA = DELIVERANCE

The cry went up as He rode into Jerusalem on the colt ...

"Hosanna! Hosanna to the Son of David! Blessed is He who comes in the name of the Lord! Hosanna in the highest!"

The people were proclaiming a prophetic truth known to them from Psalm 118:25-27. They were longing and looking for the One who would deliver them from the oppressive Roman rule. They were in literal bondage to an authority not of their choosing or liking. Their cry of "Hosanna!" was saying, "Save us now! Help us! We are imprisoned!"

The problem was, their bondage was more spiritual than physical. When we receive Jesus as Lord, He begins to reveal to us areas of life that are in bondage. There may have been a "giving over" of something to the "god of this world". Excessive eating, substance abuse, materialism, etc., are attempts to fill the hole meant only for Jesus. These things are practiced until a bondage may result, and only Jesus can really break the chains.

A spiritual bondage is often the result of a physical addiction. I'm reminded of this as I see people trying to stop destructive habits. Weight loss programs, drug and alcohol centers, and prisons, are overflowing with dear, struggling folks who would find release from their confinement if Jesus were really welcomed into their situation. If there is any bondage in your life, let this Palm Sunday be a point of release for you. Palm Sunday observes the Triumphant Entrance of Jesus into Jerusalem, a city in bondage. He wants to be the same Deliverer for all who call on His name.

Glory to the Son of David! Hosanna!

WHY NOT "EASTER SATURDAY"?

NOW ON THE FIRST DAY OF THE WEEK, MARY MAGDALENE CAME EARLY TO THE TOMB
(John 20:1)

AND EARLY ON THE FIRST DAY OF THE WEEK, THEY CAME TO THE TOMB
Mark 16:2)

NOW, AFTER THE SABBATH, AS IT BEGAN TO DAWN TOWARD THE FIRST DAY OF THE WEEK, MARY MAGDALENE AND THE OTHER MARY CAME TO LOOK AT THE GRAVE
(Matthew 28:1)

One of the dramatic things to happen as a result of the resurrection of Jesus Christ, was the change of the day of worship. The Sabbath was the Jewish day of worship. It was written into the Law and was traditionally "cast in stone". The Sabbath was not to be tampered with. It was one of the Commandments, *"Remember the Sabbath, to keep it holy."* (Exodus 20:8)

So, why did the Early Church begin to worship on Sunday? The Sabbath is Saturday and Sunday is the first day of the week, regardless of our American calendars. The above verses point out the reason ... it was the day of the Lord's miracle. He rose from the dead! That event so stirred the Believers, they literally placed their lives in danger as they changed their day of worship to celebrate the Risen Lord.

Jesus said, *"The Son of Man is Lord of the Sabbath."* A mystical saying until the Resurrection proved He was indeed the Son of God. The day of worship could not be mandated by man. For the follower of Christ, every day becomes the Holy Sabbath, and the first day of the week is when we gather to give thanks for His life. He rose that we may rise also! He lives forever that we might live forever also!

HE LIVES! HE RULES! HE REIGNS! HE IS COMING BACK AGAIN! HALLELUJAH!

It's a Variety Of Subjects From Here On!

A DAY OF DELIVERANCE

The uniqueness of Reformation Day easily escapes attention in the bristling hubub of our busy world. There are two things about the end of October Satan tries to bury, attempting to engulf us in his Halloween mess. However, he will never be able to overshadow the significance of the *Feast of Tabernacles* and *Reformation Day*.

The Feast of Tabernacles was the last of the sacred festivals under the Old Covenant (Lev.23:34; Deut.16:13). It marked the end of their harvest time and was a memorial to the time Israel wandered in the wilderness during the Exodus. During this festival, lasting seven days, the people would live in booths or tents to remind themselves of how their forefathers had to do that during their wandering.

Reformation Day marks the day Martin Luther struck the spark that changed the history of the church. It was October 31, 1517, as he marched up to the Castle Church door at Wittenberg, Germany, and there nailed his famous "95 Theses". Those 95 propositions were points to be debated, stating among other things, indulgences cannot remove sin and guilt, and in fact, are harmful. He was stating there are no "works" that will open the gate of Heaven, it is only by "Grace through faith". (Eph.2:8) It was a message of deliverance to all who were under the terrible oppression and bondage of the Roman church at that time. It pointed them to Christ and delivered them from guilt, condemnation, and fear. It was a message of freedom and hope.

Feast of Tabernacles and Reformation Day. Both are observances of deliverance from bondage. Interesting, isn't it? Satan tries to pervert this season with fear and "things that go bump in the night", but it is actually a day of Deliverance! You could shout "Hallelujah" right here! You'd think he would wise up, wouldn't you?

Celebrate Your Deliverance!

REFORMATION DAY

Today is Reformation Sunday on the Church calendar, for those who follow such things. Actually, Reformation Day is the same day as Halloween, but is observed on Sunday. These two days are such a contrast in observation and celebration.

Of course, we know about Halloween and its celebration of the occult and all things creepy. However, the Reformation was the turning point of Christendom. It was October 31, 1517, when Martin Luther nailed his 95 propositions to the door of Castle Church at Wittenberg, Germany. He wasn't just defacing property, it was the custom of the time and place to post things of interest on the church door. This event sparked the Reformation, and Protestantism was born. Luther's stand was based on God's revelation to him concerning Romans 1:17, *"The just shall live by faith"*. Here was the key to spiritual certainty. No longer would people have to labor under the law of the church, earning salvation, paying indulgences, and being oppressed by the Catholic hierarchy.

We enjoy the fruits of the Reformation. Many men and women suffered for their commitment to establish Biblical Christianity once again. Four questions that had once been a problem under Catholicism were answered in a new way, i.e.,

1. How is a person saved?
2. Where does religious authority lie?
3. What is the Church?
4. What is the essence of Christian living?

On this special day, I want to remind you the same message holds true for you. Satan still tries to push you under the rock of condemnation by insisting you aren't performing up to God's standard. Have you noticed the devil is usually the one trying to set God's standard for you? Well, not so! The "Just" still live by faith!

Rejoice in your great relationship with Jesus! It's by His Grace! And you are loved!

IT'S HIM!

John 10:13 says, "... *He calls His own sheep by name.*" In John 20:16, Jesus finds Mary Magdalene weeping at the tomb, and He said to her, *"Mary"*. He called her by her name! Why was Mary weeping? It wasn't because she knew all the doctrine concerning Jesus. Doctrine probably meant very little to her. Any Pharisee worth his salt could make a fool out of Mary doctrinally. Yet, one thing they couldn't ridicule out of her was the fact Jesus had cast seven demons from her. But even this blessing was nothing compared to an intimate relationship with Him.

Mary saw Jesus standing there and didn't realize it was Him, then He spoke to her and suddenly ... she knew! *"Rabboni! Master!"* It was Him! It is possible to know all about doctrine and yet not know Jesus. The soul itself is in danger when knowledge of doctrine steps beyond that intimate touch with Jesus. We place a strong emphasis on knowing the Word of God, and rightly so, but it must constantly launch us into fellowship with Jesus, otherwise, it is just head knowledge.

The best way to hear His voice speak your name is to spend time with Him, lots of it!

Hey, did you just hear something? Love Him with all of your heart!

JUMP, JESUS, JUMP!

AND HE SAID TO THEM, "DO NOT BE AMAZED; YOU ARE LOOKING FOR JESUS THE NAZARENE, WHO HAS BEEN CRUCIFIED. HE HAS RISEN; HE IS NOT HERE; BEHOLD, HERE IS THE PLACE WHERE THEY HAVE LAID HIM."
(Mark 16:6)

There is no statement in the life of a Christian that carries more impact than, *"He is risen!"* In that truth lies the very essence of Christianity. If that statement, and the accomplishment of it, were not a fact, there would be no Christianity, for the Risen Savior is Christianity.

A story is told of a woman who took her seven year old daughter to the main church service instead of children's church. The little girl was awed by all the things she beheld in the beautiful sanctuary. Right in the middle of the service she happened to look up and see a statue of Jesus hanging on the cross. *"Mommy, there's Jesus!"* she said out loud. *"Honey, be quiet, you're in church"*, the mother told her. *"But mommy, that's Jesus, and I want Him to come down off the cross!"* she said excitedly. Her mother whispered (being "churchy", you know) *"That's just a statue of Jesus, He's nailed to the cross so He can't come down."* The little girl looked up at the cross and shouted loudly, "JUMP, JESUS, JUMP!"

How thankful we should be that Jesus did come off the Cross. He's alive! He is risen! There is no power in any form that can keep Him nailed there! Jesus is the Living One! The Bible is so explicit about this fact, and this basic truth of Christianity should affect every facet of life!

If Jesus did not come out of the tomb, we are lost and utterly stupid ... BUT ... "HE IS RISEN, HE IS NOT HERE, BEHOLD, HERE IS THE PLACE THEY LAID HIM!"

THE TOMB IS EMPTY, HALLELUJAH!!

EMANCIPATION PROCLAMATION

In Romans 8:1-2, the Living Bible says.....

SO THERE IS NOW NO CONDEMNATION AWAITING THOSE WHO BELONG TO CHRIST JESUS. FOR THE POWER OF THE LIFE GIVING SPIRIT ... AND THIS POWER IS MINE THROUGH CHRIST JESUS ... HAS FREED ME FROM THE VICIOUS CIRCLE OF SIN AND DEATH.

If you remember your history lessons, there was a proclamation issued by President Lincoln, in September, 1862. It was called the Emancipation Proclamation. In this document, he proclaimed all slaves in any territory still at war with the Union to be free. Free! After a lifetime of slavery, abuse, and misery, they were to be released ... to live as a free people. We know this historic event became a reality only through much struggle, before and after the Proclamation.

As Christians, we experience a very similar struggle as we hear the "Emancipating Gospel". Instead of an Earthly President, we hear the voice of our Heavenly Father, saying, *"Jesus Christ sets you free!"* The Proclamation was made on the Cross. Satan wants to hide the reality of release, much as the slave owners probably did. He will do all he can to hide the truth from you. You see, he still wants your services. Well, we have news for him! He no longer has control over our lives! We are freed in Christ!

Our nation's freedom depends on our freedom in Christ. Each one of us has a part to play in history and we can only realize it as we appropriate our freedom in Christ.

The Emancipation Proclamation of our Lord Jesus Christ was signed by His blood. It is His-Story that we are no longer slaves ... we are free to walk with Him!

GOD CAN DO IT!

THEN I WILL MAKE UP TO YOU THE YEARS THE SWARMING LOCUST HAS EATEN, THE CREEPING LOCUST, THE STRIPPING LOCUST, THE GNAWING LOCUST
(Joel 2:25)

In this portion of Joel, God is promising restoration following Israel's return to Him. They had been totally devastated by a locust attack. Various kinds of locusts had stripped their land. For some people, this is an example of their lives. Through a variety of sinful practices, and a worshipping of the god of this world, they have become utterly wasted. Everything that matters to them is gone and they see no hope on the horizon.

But, maybe it wasn't quite that bad. Maybe it was just some sad spots over the years. Perhaps it was strained or broken relationships instead of love. There can be many disappointments in this world, but the Lord says it won't always be this way for those who love Him. Restoration will come. He will make up for the times of disappointment.

I too, have had letdowns and failures, however, I have learned God is a Restorer. He always makes it up somehow. As I commit to Him ... truly ... He will take care of it. Always! I feel strongly about this! I know this God's Word to us for this time. Just as God promised to restore Israel, He will restore us! There is no devastation so great that He cannot restore ... none! *"Then I will restore to you the years ..."*

Give Him your life ... let Him restore.

HE CONTINUALLY RESTORES

If there is any one thing I long for you to know and apply personally, it is that God really does love you, and will restore all things, in His time.

My thoughts have been drawn once again to the glorious words of Psalm 103. Here David gives praise, as he says;

BLESS THE LORD O MY SOUL, AND FORGET NONE OF HIS BENEFITS, WHO PARDONS ALL YOUR INIQUITIES, WHO HEALS ALL YOUR DISEASES, WHO REDEEMS YOUR LIFE FROM THE PIT, WHO CROWNS YOU WITH LOVINGKINDNESS AND COMPASSION, WHO SATISFIES YOUR YEARS WITH GOOD THINGS, SO YOUR YOUTH IS RENEWED LIKE THE EAGLE. (Ps.103:2-5)

All too often, the wonders of God are overshadowed by the rigors of life on Planet Earth. David reminds us not to forget the promises of God, and the benefits only He can offer. Always remember, God is good. He desires life, restoration, and a loving relationship with Him.

"Father, help us to sense Your lovingkindness, as we place our full weight on You. Give us the courage to allow Your precious Holy Spirit to fill us with Your presence ... healing and restoring. Amen"

May God abundantly bless and restore as you give yourself to Him ... without reservation.

Because He died for you.

Because He rose for you.

Because He's coming again ... for you.

JUST AS I AM

The words of an old hymn, say, *"If you tarry 'til you're better, you'll never come at all."* Jesus simply said ...

"COME UNTO ME ALL YOU WHO LABOR AND ARE HEAVY LADEN, AND I WILL GIVE YOU REST." (Matt.11:28)

He loves us just as we are. We need to submit to His love ... now. When the famous artist, Berta Hummel, was young, she loved to draw children. She understood young people because she was from a family of seven. Her portraits were natural looking, not an "ideal" picture of a child. She selected boys and girls from the villages near her home and sketched them just as they were, not tidied up, but with dirty faces, ragged stockings, and patched britches. She produced delightful pictures with great insight. These pictures later became the basis for her now famous Hummel figurines.

Jesus loves us just as we are, willful children, dirty faces, ragged appearances, far from the ideal. Amazingly, He doesn't demand perfection before drawing us to Himself. He doesn't put us on probation. He calls us just as we are. Yes, He will begin a process to ultimately shape us into His image, but that comes later. His drawing, His calling to Himself, is "Just As I Am".

Do we accept each other like that? What about new faces in the church? Do we pass everyone through our "Filter of Acceptance" first? Or, do we love them as they are? We should be careful to maintain a spirit of love above all else. Love for God, and love for one another, no matter what. Easy? No. God's will? Definitely.

"BELOVED, LET US LOVE ONE ANOTHER, FOR LOVE IS OF GOD."

AHHHH ... SIMPLICITY!

If there is anything I appreciate, it is having things "clear cut". I really prefer things to be open and honest, without secret agendas or guile, like this;

HE WHO HAS THE SON HAS THE LIFE; HE WHO DOES NOT HAVE THE SON OF GOD, DOES NOT HAVE THE LIFE (1 Jn.5:12)

In this Scripture, John simplifies the reality of eternal life. Either you have it ... or you don't. No guess work, no "may-bee's". Either Jesus is Lord, or He isn't. The "Life" referred to is Eternal Life, fellowship with the Father, with His Son, and with His people, found only through a personal relationship with Jesus Christ. THERE IS NO OTHER WAY.

In the Gospel of John, we find ...

HE WHO BELIEVES IN THE SON HAS ETERNAL LIFE; BUT HE WHO DOES NOT OBEY THE SON SHALL NOT SEE LIFE, BUT THE WRATH OF GOD ABIDES ON HIM. (John 3:36)

Why is this important? I believe many people are confused, lonely, and fearful. They honestly want assurance and need hope, as we all do. The problem is, there are so many philosophies and false religions available that mixed signals abound. People just don't know what to believe.

As Christians, this simple, yet awesome truth of salvation should be riveted into our heart and mind. It brings freedom and confidence, for we know God is with us! But, beyond this, what a beautiful message of hope we have to share with others! Pray for God to give you many opportunities to tell others! It's the hope people long for! It's the medicine to cure the ache in their heart! It's the love for which they long. The next chance you get to speak with someone who is struggling with life, just tell them, *"You know, a personal relationship with Jesus Christ will change your life!"*

Jesus can set them free through your faithfulness; let Him do it.

RESPONSIBILITY ... WHO NEEDS IT?

What does it mean to be responsible? It means I am accountable. It means I can tell right from wrong. It means I can act and think rationally. It means I can assume duties and obligations, being reliable and dependable. To be responsible means a lot, doesn't it? But, that's the way it is when I say, *"Jesus, You are my Lord, I want to serve You."*

With that commitment comes responsibility. I now must face some hard facts about myself, because I want to be responsible in my Christian walk. It requires me to ask questions needing answers, and it may require some action. Am I seeking God's will for my life in His Word, the Bible? Am I making definite changes in my lifestyle to conform more to what Christ desires? Am I watching my words, so they edify and encourage, instead of being negative? Do I put myself down and give in to "stinkin' thinkin'"? Am I blaming the devil about things for which I am responsible?

The list of questions may differ for each of us, but they need to be asked. We are living in a time of cleansing and responsibility for the Body of Christ. It is imperative we have an attitude of repentance because we long for God's presence in our life and in the Church.

Proverbs 18:21 says, *"Death and life are in the power of the tongue ..."* Am I killing my kids, my spouse, or myself by what I say or how I say it? Or, am I bringing life by saying and thinking God's truth? Words and thoughts of death are conceived in the womb of hell. Words and thoughts of life are born of God.

Our responsibility is to breathe life, speak life, think life, and act life. That's why Jesus came, and that's why He said, *"The thief comes only to steal, kill and destroy; I came that they might have life, and might have it abundantly."* (John 10:10)

Live with an eye for responsibility, it's His way.

WE HAVE A HERITAGE

As Christians, we can boast in our rich heritage. A heritage is something handed down from our ancestors. It can be characteristics, culture, or tradition. It can also be rights, status, or position, as we see in England's Royal Family. A heritage is something we all have, good, bad, or whatever.

Isaiah 54, lists many things about our heritage. Note how he sums it up in verse seventeen, thus ...

"NO WEAPON THAT IS FORMED AGAINST YOU SHALL PROSPER; AND EVERY TONGUE THAT ACCUSES YOU IN JUDGMENT YOU WILL CONDEMN. THIS IS THE HERITAGE OF THE SERVANTS OF THE LORD, AND THEIR VINDICATION IS FROM ME, DECLARES THE LORD".

Now, what kind of heritage is that? Well, it tells us God has made a way for us in Jesus to live our life in freedom and power ... that's part of the heritage. It tells us there is nothing Satan can develop that will result in ultimate destruction for us. What did God say? no weapon will prosper? That's what He said! Yes, there are times when everything seems to contradict this. However, we do have victory, and finally to triumph when Jesus splits the sky in His return!

When troubling thoughts try to crowd in, a weapon is being formed. When you are feeling "put out" at a brother or sister in Christ, a weapon is forming. When you feel you need to "straighten out" someone with a "Word from the Lord", a weapon is forming. There are so many ways this can happen, but that weapon cannot prosper! Remember Paul's words in 2 Corinthians 10:5;

"WE ARE DESTROYNG SPECULATIONS AND EVERY LOFTY RAISED UP AGAINST THE KNOWLEDGE OF GOD, AND WE ARE TAKING EVERY THOUGHT CAPTIVE TO THE OBEDIENCE OF CHRIST."

Let's stand together as we tear down the stronghold of Satan, and shatter the weapons. You are precious in the sight of the Lord. You are bought with His blood. You have been given His Spirit. You have been pointed toward victory in Jesus Christ ... it's your heritage! Enjoy your inheritance!

FAITH LIVING = RIGHTEOUS LIVING

Faith ... what a wonderful word that is. It is to trust, to rely on ... it is to believe.

The Old Testament doesn't use the word much, in fact, it only occurs twice in the King James Version! However, the Old Testament is full of examples of faith. It seems God figures it's more important to act like we believe than to talk about it, doesn't it?

One of the locations is Deuteronomy 32:20, and the other is Habakkuk 2:4. Let's talk about the latter, for it says;

"BEHOLD, AS FOR THE PROUD ONE, HIS SOUL IS NOT RIGHT WITHIN HIM; BUT THE RIGHTEOUS WILL LIVE BY HIS FAITH."

Now, that's a familiar principle emphasized in the New Testament by Paul and the writer of Hebrews, but they were both quoting Hab.2:4. We find it used in Romans 1:17, Galatians 3:11, and Hebrews 10:38 ... *"The righteous will live by faith."* This tells us, those made righteous by God live and survive by faith. The believer trusts God in all things.

Besides being a great statement of fact, this is also a tremendous promise. It says to me, as I learn to trust more in God, become increasingly obedient to His will, and discipline my actions to be in line with His plan for me ... I can expect faith to loom ever larger and more active in all I set out to be and do. *"Therefore, having been justified by faith ..."*. That powerful truth from Romans 5:1 is what ignited the fire in the bosom of Martin Luther. The Protestant Church exists today because of Luther's response to the message of faith. It was the hinge point of the Reformation.

Many times, faith means hanging on after all hope is gone. It can be the thrust propelling you into impossible situations, knowing things are going to turn out alright, regardless of appearances. Faith is the fuel that guarantees our journey will not end prematurely. It assures us we will make it home ... our real home!

"AND WITHOUT FAITH, IT IS IMPOSSIBLE TO PLEASE GOD, FOR HE WHO COMES TO GOD MUST BELIEVE HE IS, AND THAT HE IS A REWARDER OF THOSE WHO SEEK HIM." (Heb.11:6)

Fan the flames of your faith!

FOURTEEN STEPS TO A LIFE CHANGE

I'm so thankful God knows what we need and what will be a help to us, aren't you? Sometimes, we can get pretty intense about serving the Lord. We get involved battling Satan, we get burdened for the lost, we get angry at injustice, pornography, child abuse, etc.. We become so entrenched in these problems, so intent on the battle, we can become depleted of joy, even losing a sense of God's presence.

What can we do about it? Let me list some good ideas from Psalms 95 and 96. It will be helpful for you to read these Psalms together, then consider ...

1. Sing for joy.
2. Shout joyfully.
3. Come before His presence.
4. Worship and bow down.
5. Don't harden your heart.
6. Sing a new song.
7. Proclaim His salvation.
8. Tell of His glory.
9. Ascribe to the Lord the glory due His name.
10. Bring an offering.
11. Come into His courts.
12. Worship the Lord (Again!)
13. Tremble before Him.
14. Say, "The Lord reigns!"

I have a pretty strong hunch, if we would <u>do</u> what the Psalmist says, we would experience a marked change in attitude, motive, and desire. We were created to worship and glorify God. When we do it, I believe it makes God very happy, don't you?

I encourage you to read these two Psalms, meditate on them, then ... try it!

You are loved!

A WOMAN'S LOT

The life of a woman has not always been an easy one. (Did I hear a feminine "Amen"?) The Bible gives much insight, both positive and negative, concerning the role of women.

On the positive side, let's note some history shaping events;

- Women were not God's afterthought. Men and women together are the image of God. (Gen.1:26-27)

- Jochabed took the initiative to save her son, Moses, from the murder decree of Pharoah.(Exod.2)

- Hannah made an aggressive covenant with God. (1Sam.1:1-25)

- Deborah was a judge that helped lead an army. (Judges 4:6-9)

These are but a few. There was also Miriam, Esther, Ruth, Mary, Martha, Sarah, Rahab, etc. Many women were honored for their faith, and I believe many more since would qualify for the "Ladies Hall of Faith". However, women also had some obstacles; in fact, there was a Jewish prayer of first century men thanking God for not making them women! Also consider;

- Normally, only men could own property. A daughter may inherit only if there were no sons. (Num.27:8)

- A wife could keep a promise only if the husband allowed it. (Num.30:10)

- If a woman failed to have a child, it was considered a sign of God's disapproval, and her fault. (Gen.30:1-2,22)

- Women were expected to prove their virginity. (Deut.22:20)

  - A woman's life was considered to have half the monetary value of a man's life. (Lev.27:1-8)

An extensive study of Biblical women would reveal much more, and today it is obvious a woman's life is still not simple. Many of the Old Testament ways have given way to new expressions, and in our contemporary context, "Westernized".

The coming of Jesus established new freedom for women. He launched the true E.R.A. Movement as He sat in the Synagogue and read from Isaiah; *"He has sent Me to proclaim release to the captives"*

Ladies, God has created you to be a woman, with all that implies. I would encourage you to resist the pressure of the world to be other than what God has created you to be.

You are a gift from God!

STABLE? ... YOU BET!

So ... how much did you lose in the stock market crash? The news has been interesting this week, hasn't it? Can you relate to losing a trillion dollars? I'm not sure I even know how many zeroes that is. The news media have been proclaiming this "slide" is greater than the "Big One" of '29.

I certainly don't like to see trouble in our nation, however, I can't help but rejoice as I'm reminded of the stability found only in a relationship with God through Jesus Christ. God has always been, and will eternally be the only thing stable. There is nothing that will last forever except the things of the Lord. He is always there! Because God is stable, He enables us to have stability also.

Hebrews 10:23, says ...

LET US HOLD FAST THE CONFESSION OF OUR HOPE WITHOUT WAVERING, FOR HE WHO PROMISED IS FAITHFUL

We are able to be stable in a confession of hope. Knowing Jesus plants hope securely in the heart, and then, we have a message of hope for others. Your stability can touch others and give them hope, because they see your newfound steadfastness. They knew you when you weren't stable, now they can see that you are, and you can give God the glory. He gets the credit! Isn't that wonderful?

Because Jesus lives, we live also. Because we live in Him, others can live also as God uses your life to touch someone else. I rejoice when I see stability happening in others, and in myself. It isn't always easy, but God understands that. He is patient with us. We must be patient also, a masterpiece can take some time to be formed, and Christians are His workmanship you know.

THEREFORE, MY BELOVED BRETHREN, BE STEADFAST, IMMOVABLE, ALWAYS ABOUNDING IN THE WORK OF THE LORD, KNOWING YOUR TOIL IS NOT IN VAIN IN THE LORD.
(1 Corinthians 15:58)

Be rooted, riveted, and anchored in Him.

A MORE IMPORTANT TREASURE

Lately, there's been much attention focused on the finding of the Titanic, the great ship that tragically sunk in the North Atlantic many years ago. Hundreds of lives were lost, bringing grief into homes around the world as people mourned such a loss.

I find it interesting, though not surprising, so much publicity is given to the artifacts retrieved from the ocean floor. It is fascinating to see the various items; dishes, personal effects, parts of the steering and navigational instruments, etc. Research can be very intriguing.

However, all of this rekindles within my spirit a renewed sense of value and priority. The "world" sees recovered treasure, such as the Titanic, as a great prize ... and don't forget the profit many will enjoy.

As a Christian, I find it interesting, but my treasure is in Heaven. My priority is to be my relationship with Jesus Christ. We don't really need to worry about those things that will corrode and rust away. We all have to work at that, don't we?

Many times, I have seen a new, shiny car roll into the shop for an estimate to repair damage. The owner often has to make some adjustments as he sees this $25,000.00 treasure deteriorating before his eyes. *"It'll never be the same!"* he cries inside ... and sometimes he cries it outside! He's right, it will never be the same. Oh, it can be repaired so nobody could detect it, but it has been damaged, and nothing can change that.

Our concern needs to be about where <u>our</u> treasure is. It should be in Heaven, not lying on the ocean floor, rotting away in the dark.

Here is a treasure worth going for;

PURSUE PEACE WITH ALL MEN, AND THE SANCTIFICATION WITHOUT WHICH NO ONE WILL SEE THE LORD. (Hebrews 12:14)

Peace and Sanctification (holiness) won't rust away. Look to Jesus.

BUT I'M ONLY A ---

How would you complete that thought? What are you "Only"?
1 Corinthians 1:27-28 says;

"GOD HAS CHOSEN THE FOOLISH THINGS, THE WEAK THINGS, THE BASE THINGS, AND THE DESPISED, THE THINGS THAT ARE NOT"

The reason for this is found in verse twenty-nine, *"... that no man should boast before God."* It was God's desire to use the things, the circumstances and the people the world considered of little account. He chose the simple to confound and shame the wise. Not because He wants anyone to be humiliated because they are educated or have special abilities ... God loves smart and gifted people, too. He desires the glory to be His, not ours. God's will is for us to give Him credit that is due Him.

Whatever good we have accomplished, whatever ability we may have developed, whatever giftedness we may have, be it great or small, is due to His grace and mercy. It is His empowering, His wisdom, His ability to guide, His strength, His courage, His provision, and His love, that has placed us in the enviable position we find ourselves.

You may say, *"But, I have nothing to be envied!"* If you have a relationship with Jesus Christ, you are blessed. That position can be envied by every person in the world who doesn't have such contact with Heaven. They could lament, *"O' how I wish I had your peace, your joy, your hope!"*

Yes, you may feel you don't have much to offer, but thanks be to God ... that's His choice! And besides, your opinion of yourself is just that ... your opinion. Look in the Bible to see what God thinks of you. You could begin with Ephesians 1:3-14 & 2:4-10.

God can use you! He <u>chose</u> you! Be thankful!

TAKING CAPTIVES

TAKE CAPTIVE EVERY THOUGHT TO MAKE IT OBEDIENT TO CHRIST
(2 Cor.10:5)

Ah, the thoughts of a person ... what a tremendous arena! It is there we enjoy journeys to the far reaches of the universe. It is there we can experience what may never come to pass in reality. Within the kingdom of the mind is the ability to alter the course of our life, and the life of others. God has created in each of us an unsurpassed computer. What man will never be able to better, God created with a Word. The mind is a constant source of wonder, of joy, of pleasant things, of dreams, and ...oh, oh, can also become the "devil's playground". If there is one common battle we all share, it is the war waged in the mind, our thought life. We must continually confront it, faithfully shaping this area of life to conform to Christ.

2 Corinthians 10:5, tells me there is hope;
"We are taking captive every thought to make it obedient to Christ."

Satan filters his thoughts into your mind occasionally, and if we allow them to grow as he wants, we literally come into bondage, a prisoner. Yet, Paul says we are to take the thoughts captive. That's right! Jesus in you has the authority and the ability to tear down the stronghold. You don't have to be the captive ... you can make Satan the captive!

As we obey God in our thoughts, the walk of victory is ours, we are in control! Don't ever think you're the only one who has this type of struggle, none of us is exempt. It almost seems to be a rule, doesn't it? The more you want to serve the Lord, the more Satan tries to establish a stronghold in your mind.

Are you relating to this? Sure you are. Don't worry, you don't have to put up with it ... take it captive!

You are His masterpiece!

NEWNESS AND FAITH

Another new year! So, what are going to do differently this year? That takes some thought, doesn't it? I wonder if anyone actually keeps New Year's resolutions. However, it is a good time to think about newness.

The Bible has a lot to say about "Newness". One of the benefits of Christianity is that we don't have to muddle around in the "Old", we are "New" in Jesus Christ! He and He alone can make all things new!

Paul writes, in Ephesians 4:22-24 ff

"IN REFERENCE TO YOUR FORMER MANNER OF LIFE ... BE RENEWED IN THE SPIRIT OF YOUR MIND, AND PUT ON THE NEW SELF, WHICH, IN THE LIKENESS OF GOD, HAS BEEN CREATED IN RIGHTEOUSNESS AND HOLINESS OF TRUTH."

Paul says, "Put on the new self". What would you like to put on this year? God will honor your desire to be formed to His likeness. You can always count on God's help if your desire is to become more like Him. Me? I'm looking to put on more faith, more trust in my Lord Jesus. I want to experience faith deeper than ever before. Faith is a funny thing isn't it? We're often sure we don't have any, yet, our lives are filled with acts of faith every day. Did you ever think of that?

How often have you gone through an automatic door, such as at the grocery store? As you walked briskly toward it, how did you know it would open? Faith! How often do you eat or drink from a sealed container of some sort, like a soft drink or canned food? How did you know it was o.k.? Faith! In traveling to an unknown destination, you may have used a road map. How did you know you would arrive at the right place? Faith! When you get in your car, how do you know it will start and take you where you want to go? (Oh, you have one of those cars, too?) Now, that's really faith! Ever use an elevator? How did you know it would go up ... or down? Faith! Ever fly in an airplane or ride in a boat, etc., etc.? It all takes a measure of faith, doesn't it?

Yes, we learn to take things for granted, but all these experiences should prove to us faith is not a foreigner, we are people of faith. I am praying my faith in God's Word will increase, greatly! Of course, as with the aforementioned examples, faith means acting as if it will happen ... like walking through the grocer's door.

Expecting faith growth is like is a little like praying for patience ... it takes opportunities for it to happen to bring it to reality. Learn to trust God this year for great things, to His glory, and so you may become better equipped for His service.

Faith is the victory!

DOING THE WORK OF GOD

Do you ever have a desire to "work" for God? Most card-carrying Christians would probably say, *"Sure, who wouldn't want to work for God?"* But, what is His work? How would you answer that? Well, let's see, there's preaching, teaching, witnessing, Bible study, cleaning the church, helping people, being a missionary, raising children in the Lord, etc., etc.. All these things are good, and can be works of the Lord, but there is a work superceding all this.
Let's see what Jesus said in John 6:28-29 ...

THEY SAID THEREFORE TO HIM, WHAT SHALL WE DO THAT WE MAY DO THE WORKS OF GOD? JESUS ANSWERED, AND SAID TO THEM, THIS IS THE WORK OF GOD, THAT YOU BELIEVE IN HIM WHO HE HAS SENT.

<u>Being a Believer is the work of God</u>. Of course, this implies a lot, doesn't it? But, this is the foundation to it all. Consider some observations about believing:

Being a Believer is not ...
- Blindly following anything coming in the name of Jesus.
- Letting someone else think for me.
- Pretending everything is o.k..
- Putting on a religious front.

Believing in Jesus is ...
- Taking down barriers to God.
- Refusing to be critical of others.
- Knowing God is not limited to my interpretation of life or circumstances.
- Taking an active part in my Christian maturing process.

When Jesus said to "Believe", it was surprising to many who were gathered there. This wasn't the definition they expected, or wanted to hear. At this point for many of the followers, Believing became too much work and they left Him. They weren't willing to pay the price of belief. Believing can be hard work at times. It isn't always easy or simple, but ... it is the "Work" of God.
"Believe in the Lord Jesus Christ, and you shall be saved." (Acts 16:31)
Working ... Believing, together with you!

CONTENTMENT ... AHHHHH!

LET YOUR CHARACTER BE FREE FROM THE LOVE OF MONEY, BEING CONTENT WITH WHAT YOU HAVE
(Hebrews 13:5)

FOR I LEARNED TO BE CONTENT IN WHATEVER CIRCUMSTANCES I AM
(Phil.4:11)

GODLINESS IS A MEANS OF GREAT GAIN, WHEN ACCOMPANIED BY CONTENTMENT
(1Tim 6:6)

What a wonderful place to be! How great it is to be contented! As I say this, you may be thinking, *"Oh sure, that's fine for you to say, you don't know my troubles!"*

Isn't this one of the reasons we're not contented? We are just sure everyone else is satisfied, having no problems, everything is wonderful and they are doing fine. *"But ... things never seem to go right for me!"* Sound familiar? I want to encourage you to be content. I mean, right now, regardless of circumstances. It doesn't mean giving up, it doesn't mean things can't change, it doesn't mean burying your head in the sand, pretending all is o.k. when it isn't.

It does mean, <u>being content</u>, knowing God is a very real, vital force in your life, and He will see that you make it! God is helping us grow through each experience of life. Our stress usually comes because we aren't getting our way...hmmmmm. That's a little hard to admit, isn't it? It is for me, too. However, it is one of the main reasons for a lack of contentment.

When our attitude becomes one of gratitude, we find we can be content ... no matter what. Remember, God is FOR you!

May you be contented with Jesus!

BLESSED ARE THE MEEK ... THEY TRUST GOD

I thought you might enjoy this excerpt from *"I Never Promised You A Hot-tub"*:

"Russian novelist, Leo Tolstoy, wrote a short story about a bishop who visited a tiny island where three, poor, uneducated men of God lived alone. The three old men only knew one prayer ... *'Three are Ye, three are we, have mercy on us!* I see you wish to please the Lord, but you don't know how', said the bishop. 'That is not the way to pray.' So, the bishop spent the day teaching the men the Lord's Prayer. They learned slowly, but by night, they could recite the prayer. Hours after the bishop had said his farewell to the men and set sail for his home, he and his crew saw what they thought was a ship sailing after them. They soon realized though that it was, as Tolstoy put it, 'the three hermits running upon the water, all gleaming white, their grey beards shining, and approaching the ship as quickly as though it were not moving.' Stopping within shouting distance of the ship, the hermits called to the bishop. They had forgotten the Lord's Prayer, and wanted him to teach them the words again. Humbled by the faith of these men, the bishop told them their own prayer would reach the Lord. *'It is not for me to teach'*, he said, *'pray for us sinners.'*

Meekness means total dependence on God, a quality the bishop saw in these men. They had the faith to run across waves, yet they did not do it to impress others, they did it to ask for more teaching. The hermits had few clothes, and very little intelligence, but they were meek enough to know they had all they needed.

Matthew 5:5: *BLESSED ARE THE MEEK, FOR THEY SHALL INHERIT THE EARTH* ...is a promise for those who learn to walk by faith, as the three hermits.

We will see a day when the People of God, the "Meek", will take over the land, reclaiming what Satan has kept in bondage and chaos. We must be people who are intent on righteousness and faith. We must become praying, sin-hating, God-loving people, if we are to be effective in reaching the lost for Jesus Christ.

THE HUMBLE WILL INHERIT THE LAND, AND WILL DELIGHT THEMSELVES IN ABUNDANT PROSPERITY. (Psalm 37:11)

YESTERDAY, TODAY, AND TOMORROW

Allow me to share an article with you I recently received from my father. It's food for thought;

"There are two days in every week about which we should not worry ... two days which can be kept free from fear and apprehension. One of these days is yesterday, with its mistakes and cares, its aches and pains, its faults and blunders. Yesterday has passed forever beyond our control. The entire world cannot bring back yesterday. We cannot undo a single act we performed, we cannot erase a single word we said. Yesterday is gone.

The other day we should not worry about is tomorrow, with its possible adversities, its burdens, its large promise and poor performance. Tomorrow also is beyond our immediate control. Tomorrow's sun will rise, either in splendor, or in a mask of clouds ... but, it will rise. Until it does, we have no stake in tomorrow, it is yet unborn.

That leaves only one day ... today. Any man can fight the battles of just one day. It is only when you and I add the burden of those two awful eternities. yesterday and tomorrow, that we break down.

It is not the experience of today that drives men mad, it is remorse or bitterness for something which happened yesterday, and the dread of what tomorrow may bring. Let us, therefore, journey but one day at a time."

This may sound a little fatalistic, but it has merit in the light of Scripture. The New Testament teaches us not to fear ---
1 Peter 5:7, says to, *"Cast your care on Him, for He cares for you."*
Luke 12:31, tells us, *"Seek first the kingdom of God and His righteousness ..."*

God has a wonderful way of healing the yesterdays, preparing the tomorrows, and empowering us for the today's.

Remember, only things promised by God are inevitable, He has a way of changing everything else for His glory.

TIME TO FACE THE TRUTH

I recently read an article with the above title, written by a charismatic Lutheran pastor. He spoke of the need to call sin what it is ... sin. He pointed out how we are given to "euphemisms", i.e., a pleasing expression used in place of one which is plainer and more accurate, but which may be offensive. For example, we don't have much adultery or fornication anymore, we now have premarital or extramarital sex. Instead of homosexuality, we now have "gay" or "alternate-lifestyle". These words have a cleaner and more clinical flavor. You get the picture.

This is really the way things seem today, and yes, we do need to face up to reality. However, to move this concept a little further along, I suggest we face the truth about the ground we've gained also. Acknowledging the reality of our sinfulness is important, but let's also accept the growth and change for good in our lives. I find many Christians are quick to believe they are a worm of the lowest class, but they aren't easily convinced they are growing and being shaped in to the image of Christ ... and it actually shows! A saint? Me? Oh, I'm not so sure ... Well, face this truth ---

WE ARE HIS WORKMANSHIP, CREATED IN CHRIST JESUS FOR GOOD WORKS ... REMEMBER THAT FORMERLY, YOU THE GENTILES ... WERE SEPERATE FROM CHRIST ... EXCLUDED ... STRANGERS ... HAVING NO HOPE AND WITHOUT GOD ... BUT, NOW IN CHRIST JESUS, HAVE BEEN BROUGHT NEAR BY THE BLOOD OF CHRIST ...
(Excerpts of Ephesians 2:10-13)

Yes, we were lost, without hope ... dead. But, now, if you trust in Jesus Christ, and Him alone for your salvation, you are made alive, a new creation! Sure you were rotten! Who wasn't? But, the blood of Jesus cleanses us and sets us free! His Holy Spirit enables us to walk in obedience to His Word ... and one day soon, we will see Jesus!

Let's face it ... Jesus is Tremendous!

IMPRESSIVE COMMITMENT

Do you know someone who really impresses you? I mean, someone besides Jesus. You know, a person who stands firm in the face of opposition. A person of character, a person you admire, one with whom you would associate.

The one who stands out for me, is the apostle, Paul. One of the main reasons for which I admire him is found in 1 Corinthians 2:1-2, where he says;

AND WHEN I CAME TO YOU, BRETHREN, I DID NOT COME WITH SUPERIORITY OF SPEECH OR OF WISDOM, PROCLAIMING TO YOU THE TESTIMONY OF GOD. FOR I DETERMINED TO KNOW NOTHING AMONG YOU EXCEPT CHRIST, AND HIM CRUCIFIED.

Paul, the expert Pharisee, sophisticated, intelligent, wise, educated, gifted, courageous, chosen of God to preach to a pagan Gentile world. He made a decision to set aside the credentials of the world and proclaim the basic Gospel message. That impresses me.

I've noticed it is becoming increasingly unpopular to take a definite stand on issues. If you are a person who strives to maintain an absolute standard, especially for Christ, you may be labeled, "Radical", or "Fanatic", or worse. Instead of being accepted as a person of integrity and principle, you become a thorn in the flesh of those desiring a liberal, humanistic world.

But ... all who commit to The Way, the Servanthood of Christ, and aggressively live it, will understand Paul's position. We too, must *"know nothing except Christ, and Him crucified."*

The simplicity of the Gospel must be maintained, even as we mature in Him. Yes, we study, we learn, we grow in excellence, but we must never lose sight of the truth setting men free from the claws of Satan. Jesus came to set captives free!

We are more than conquerors, we are overcomers, victorious in Jesus!

ARE YOU "STRESSED"?

Among the most popular "buzz words" of our day is the word, "Stress". It seems to be on everyone's mind and in their conversation. With the economic pressures we face, the onslaught of AIDS, the battle for the environment, the delicate nature of the nuclear world around us, the breakdown of families, etc., we are forced into a pressure-cooker existence. The result of this phenomena is stress.

I suppose we've all seen or heard at least one of the many studies on the subject. One thing is certain. It's practically impossible to escape stress. However, what I'm hearing is that pressure isn't the problem. The manner in которой we react, is. A key factor is hostility. If you respond to pressure with anger or bitterness, or in some other negative fashion, you may suffer the consequences. *"Be angry ... sin not."* Still good counsel, isn't it?

As Christians, we must remember there are built-in "Stress-relievers" in the Bible.

Note 1 Thessalonians 5:16-18

REJOICE ALWAYS ... PRAY WITHOUT CEASING ... IN EVERYTHING GIVE THANKS, FOR THIS IS GOD'S WILL FOR YOU IN CHRIST JESUS.

If the strain of living in this world seems bigger than life at times, remember who, and whose, you are. You are a child of the King! You have the resources of Heaven at your disposal!

Be "cool" in Jesus!

IT WILL PASS

AND IT CAME TO PASS THAT EVERYONE WHO CALLS ON THE NAME OF THE LORD WILL BE SAVED (Acts 2:21)

If you were to explore your Bible from cover to cover, you would read, *"It came to pass"*, hundreds of times. The above verse Peter quoted from Joel, is certainly one of the best examples of this.

In this prophetic Word, I see two things to consider;

- It will come to pass that I will need to call on the name of the Lord.

- As I am saved, my crisis will have come to pass, not stay.

We must remember, God is aware we have need of Him. He also realizes there are times when we think we don't need Him. But, God is the author of *"It came to pass"*, and sure enough, it will *"Come to pass"*.

So there we sit, being slightly overwhelmed by the latest trial that blew into our life. After we've exhausted all our tricks, we finally "call on the name of the Lord". (Phew!) Now things begin to change. Somehow, circumstances look different than they did yesterday. A week later, we wonder what all the worry was about, then we realize, *"It came to pass"* ... it didn't come to stay! Praise God! We didn't have to stay in the midst of the trial! It's a sure thing in the Lord. It's guaranteed. It's His promise. If we call on Him ... we will be saved!

Now, that's what the Bible says. Whatever you are facing, whatever you will be facing ... will pass. Just as it "came to pass", it will continue, right on past. Escapism? Stoicism? Not at all. It is trusting in the only One able to see us through. He is the One who allowed it to come to pass in the first place.

Look to Jesus ... it will pass.

MR. ORDINARY

"I'm so ... so ... so, ordinary! All around me are these gifted, excellent, people, but look at me! Ordinary!"

Sound familiar? At the outset, let me tell you, Scripture does a great job proving God uses ordinary people. "Name one", you say? Okay, how about Andrew? Andrew was the original "Mr. Ordinary" of the New Testament.

Consider these facts about him:

- First of the Twelve to follow Jesus, but never became "prominent".

- Brother of Simon Peter, yet not included in the "Inner Circle".

- Regularly identified as Peter's brother, but Peter was never identified as Andrew's brother. *"Andrew? Oh, you mean the tag-a-long, Peter's brother?"*

- Andrew wrote no epistles.

- No miracles attributed to Andrew.

- Not an eloquent preacher like his brother.

- Rarely, if ever, in the foreground, and definitely not a leader.

However, today his name is used by the Billy Graham Association as the title for their evangelism outreach. "Operation Andrew" came about because Andrew was the Evangelist who brought his brother to Jesus.

Traditionally, Andrew has become the patron saint of at least three cultures. He was considered the first missionary north of the Black Sea, so the Russians claim him. Greek tradition claims him because it's said he was martyred there on an X shaped cross, where he hung for three days praying for his captors. Also, the white Saint Andrews cross on a blue background is the standard for Scotland.

Why would three nations claim, "Mr. Ordinary"? Because, in the Gospels, Andrew's name implies caring evangelism. "Ordinary" Andrew simply and caringly brought people to Christ.

Notice a few of his qualities:

- He thought of others first. (John 1:40-42)

- He was optimistic about what Jesus could do.(John 6:5-9)

- He believed Jesus was for everyone. (John 15:20-22)

At the root of his virtues, lies ordinariness. He knew his human inadequacy, which fostered his dependence on God and made him extra-ordinarily useful to God. God uses ordinary people to do extra-ordinary work for Him. Are you ordinary? You are? Wonderful!

SMILE AS YOU GO UNDER

"There must be some way to use this", I thought to myself. On the license frame of a pickup I was repairing was the statement, *"If you're sinking, smile as you go under!"*

I thought, *"This is the attitude of a stoic, for sure!"* I suppose we've all had times when we felt our ship was about to go down. The last thing we felt like doing was to smile.

To smile would mean;

- I'm a faith-packed powerhouse
    --- or ---
- I'm an idiot who doesn't really grasp the dilemma.

I confess I have fallen into both categories on occasion. How about you? But! ... However! ... Ahah! ... We have a God who won't allow us to sink ... smiling or not!

Isaiah 40:31 tells us ...

THOSE WHO WAIT FOR THE LORD WILL GAIN NEW STRENGTH; THEY WILL MOUNT UP WITH WINGS LIKE EAGLES, THEY WILL RUN AND NOT GET TIRED, THEY WILL WALK AND NOT BECOME WEARY.

God's priority for us to pray and seek Him. If we are sincerely doing that, we won't sink, I promise. But keep smilin' any way ... it looks good on ya!

WHY BOTHER?

Have you ever asked yourself, "Why bother to tell anyone about Jesus?" Sometimes, in the midst of the world's pressures and attractions, the intensity of the need to share the Gospel can wane. As a reminder, let me parade a few thoughts past you of our vital responsibility, viz.:

- The reality of Hell. How's that for starters? In Luke 16:23, the rich man sees Abraham from his place in Hades, and longs to share the pleasant situation he beholds ... to no avail. A sad story, but Hell is real.
- We have the message of Life, not death.
- We have the only remedy. Read John 14:6, *"No one comes to the Father but through Me"* (Jesus).
- We are commanded to witness. Acts 1:8, and 1 Peter 3:15.
- We have been appointed. John 15:16 *"I chose you, and appointed you that you should go ..."*
- Because of the reward awaiting us. 2 Timothy 4:8, says, *"In the future there is laid up for me a crown of righteousness."* Jesus was a soul winner. Luke 19:10, says, *"The Son of Man came to seek and save that which was lost."*
- Because of the desperate need of perishing people. John 3:36 says, *"He who believes in the Son has eternal life; but he who does not obey the Son shall not see life, but the wrath of God rests on him."*

We could add many more reasons to this list, couldn't we? The fact remains, we have been given a tremendous Gospel, "Good News" to share with the world. The life He has put in you, He wants to place within others. You have a real message of hope the world needs to hear.

Are you telling it?

AN IMPORTANT HEALING

Throughout the New Testament, we see the healing power of Jesus reach into the lives of many people. Many were touched by the personal ministry of the Master Physician Himself. Many more were healed as Jesus worked through His servants ... people who believed and were available, people of faith. When we think of healing, we automatically connect that to sick bodies or troubled minds.

However, there is a healing mentioned in Jeremiah I find very noteworthy, i.e.,:

RETURN O' FAITHLESS SONS, I WILL HEAL YOUR FAITHLESSNESS. BEHOLD WE CAME TO THEE; FOR THOU ART THE LORD, OUR GOD.
(Jeremiah 3:22)

God told Israel He would heal their faithlessness, if they would repent ... which they did. Walking a course differing from what God intends will result in a loss of faith, a breaking, or even a "sickness" of faith. If there is repentance, God will heal this malady. Our confession is to be as Israel's when they turned again ... *"For Thou art the Lord, our God."*

How is your faith? Are you being obedient to the Lord, according to His Word? He will heal your faithlessness just as He heals your body. He is *"Jehovah-Rapha, the Lord, our Healer"!* This is an exciting day, indeed! There are hundreds of people in our community who need healing, healing of physical things, emotional problems, sin, etc.. Jesus is present to heal!

Now, don't you think when those two factors meet, something ought to happen? I do ... and I want to be there! Don't you?

WHAT ARE YOU REALLY WORTH?

Because of my experience in repairing automobiles, I'm asked occasionally, *"How much is this thing worth, anyhow?"* Actually, I usually don't know, because a car, or anything else, is only as valuable as what someone will pay for it. A new Mercedes isn't worth two cents if nobody wants to buy it.

People often measure the value of their lives by their looks or talents, what they have done, or haven't done. They say, "I'm valuable", or, "I'm not valuable", based on these shallow and imprecise guidelines.

How valuable are you? In 1 Corinthians 6:20 and 7:23, the Bible says, *"You were bought with a price."* It also says in 1 Peter 1:19, 2 Peter 2:1, and Revelation 5:9, that price was, *"The precious blood of Jesus."*

You are worth the price of the Son of God! Think of it! You are worth the blood of the Lord Jesus Christ! That is far greater than silver and gold, or looks, or talents, or accomplishments. Remember to remind the devil of that fact the next time he tells you your life doesn't amount to much.

You are valuable!

I'M SURE YOU CAN RELATE

It was "lump in the throat" time again, as the huge DC-10 was pushed back from the loading gate. Sitting on the apron, its engines began screaming to life, and I was becoming increasingly aware of a strong desire to rush out there with my arms waving, yelling, *"Wait! Wait! She's not going with you!"* As I thought this, I was also aware there would be someone appear on the scene to haul me off to who knows where, forcing Martha to arrange for visiting hours.

Ever have times like this? Sure you have. If you're a parent, you know what I mean because you've been there. That gigantic airplane contained a precious treasure as it began the first leg of a journey that would deposit our daughter, Susan, in Guatemala, placing her totally out of our reach. If she needs anything, we won't be able to be there. When our son, Tony, married Irene, the same experience happened. Suddenly, you realize your ability to be there for those you love so dearly can only reach so far.

Our real dependence must be on God. He is the only One. He is the only Way. These are the times when a deep, personal relationship with Jesus Christ brings joy, instead of sorrow. Hope, instead of discouragement, for as He said, *"I will never desert you, nor will I ever forsake you."*

Don't be fearful of trusting God to care for those who are dear to your heart. He knows your love and concern for them.

You see ... He also had a Son He loved.

HOORAY FOR JOB!

In Job we see a classic example of two things not enjoyed by many ... suffering and patience.

When we think of Job, we visualize a poor, tattered guy sitting on an ash heap, scraping his boil covered body with a piece of broken pottery. His patience in waiting for God's intervention challenges us to new heights of faith and trust in God's grace. Alas, Job had no support group. In Job 2:9, even his wife said to him, *"Do you still hold fast to your integrity? Curse God and die!"* Some support, huh? Notice Job's reply, *"Shall we indeed accept good from God and not accept adversity? In all this, Job did not sin with his lips."*(Job 2:10) What a guy!

I will boldly say, anyone who lives a life committed to Christ will suffer adversity in some manner because of that commitment. It comes with the package. Problems and afflictions will come, but the focus should center on how we deal with them. If we blame God or other people, we will miss what God desires for us.

What was Job's outcome? His trial ended with God's blessing of more than he had before. Much more. Even more important than the material blessings Job received, was the prophetic insight given him. In the midst of pain and the attempted annihilation by his "friends", Job maintained, *"As for me, I know that my Redeemer lives, and at the last He will take His stand on the earth."*(Job 19:25) Job knew God was in control, and his future was in the hands of his Redeemer.

Whatever trials we face, let's learn from Job's experience. However bad it may seem, we have a God who knows exactly where we are, what we are doing, and what the outcome will be. If we learn to focus on our Redeemer, we will have blessing and provision. Is it easy to do? No. Can it be done in our high-tech world so different from Job's? Absolutely. God hasn't changed, and He never will.

Keep your eyes on Jesus ... you will be alright.

SO, WHAT IS REALLY IMPORTANT?

What is really important? That question can have a lot of answers, can't it? What may be tremendously important to me may be insignificant to someone else. Things that seem important have a way of arranging themselves according to priority as our desires change. Importance is affected by so many factors ... our needs, our wants, our opinions, our commitments, our relationships, etc.. When my sense of what is important gets a little cloudy, the Lord may direct me to a Scripture like 1 Corinthians 15:3-4:

FOR I DELIVERED TO YOU AS OF FIRST IMPORTANCE WHAT I ALSO RECEIVED, THAT CHRIST DIED FOR OUR SINS, ACCORDING TO THE SCRIPTURES, AND THAT HE WAS BURIED, AND THAT HE WAS RAISED ON THE THIRD DAY, ACCORDING TO THE SCRIPTURES

What is important? What is of first importance? Paul, the Apostle, says the Gospel should be number one. There are horrendous needs in the world for food, medicine, clothing, etc., legitimate needs for sure. But, are they <u>most</u> important? As we pray for missions, at home and abroad, we must not lose sight of the importance of the proclamation of the Gospel of Jesus Christ. Empty stomachs are certainly to be cared for, sick and broken bodies definitely need our attention, but these needs cannot be of first importance. That space must be filled with the Eternal-Life giving message of the Gospel.

Don't let Satan convince you it really doesn't matter ... it's the only thing that does matter!

KEEP ON TRACK

BELOVED, DO NOT BELIEVE EVERY SPIRIT, BUT TEST THE SPIRITS TO SEE WHETHER THEY ARE FROM GOD; BECAUSE MANY FALSE PROPHETS HAVE GONE INTO THE WORLD (1 Jn.4:1)

LET NO ONE IN ANY WAY DECEIVE YOU (2 THESS.2:3)

FOR FALSE CHRISTS AND FALSE PROPHETS WILL ARISE AND SHOW GREAT SIGNS AND WONDERS, SO AS TO MISLEAD, IF POSSIBLE, THE ELECT (MATTHEW 24:24)

On my bulletin board there is posted a quotation from the Reader's Digest, stating, *"The difference between genius and stupidity is that genius has it's limits."*

False doctrine and stupidity have a lot in common. It doesn't take much of a scholar to realize there are many opportunities available for one to stray into the pit called "Heresy". Religion is so important to mankind, validity and truth sometimes takes a back seat. If it feels good, appeals to my ego, seems logical, is espoused by some celebrity, is currently popular, etc., then it must be alright ... is the philosophy that keeps counselors trying to patch up broken lives.

The Christian life is not as complex and difficult as Satan would have us believe. Man has always had a gift for complicating what God has created in simplicity. I love to dig and research a Biblical truth, which is good, but if it is forced beyond the intended meaning it can become false teaching ... not so good.

It is necessary for all Believers to "rightly divide the Word". Be careful about accepting every new teaching, or teacher, that comes your way. Be in the Bible often; be on your knees a lot. Be faithful and diligent in your attendance at church. Remember, the Gospel is able to lead you through anything you face.

Use it wisely and often.

KEEPING FULL

Paul, the apostle, writes, *"... And do not get drunk with wine, which leads to debauchery. Instead, be filled with the Spirit."* (Ephesians 5:18)

A little study of the people in the Early Church of the Book of Acts reveals they had renewed "fillings" with the Holy Spirit. (Acts 2:4, 4:8,31; 9:17; 13:9) This doesn't imply the Holy Spirit has a lack of commitment to us, a coming and going. It is really an indication people have a tendency to "leak". He comes and abides (1John 2:27). Yet, there is a real human bent toward losing the sense of His presence at times. There is a "drain-off" occurring through the stress of daily living. (Does it help to know you're not the only one?)

Paul's words, *"Be filled with the Spirit"*, literally say, *"Be continually being filled"!* It is a command, an imperative. But how do I maintain this fellowship? This is a vital question isn't it?

There is a pattern of life insuring a continual "fullness" of His Spirit realized through these three basic disciplines

1. Worship and praise

2. Feeding on the Word of God (Scripture)

3. Faithful obedience to His Word

Sounds terribly simplistic, doesn't it? God never intended relationship with Him to be complicated, we make it that way. I assure you, if these three basics become part of your daily living, there's no reason you ever need be less than "Full of faith and the Holy Ghost." (Acts 6:5)

OMNI?

WHERE CAN I GO FROM YOUR SPIRIT? WHERE CAN I FLEE FROM YOUR PRESENCE? IF I GO TO THE HEAVENS, YOU ARE THERE; IF I MAKE MY BED IN SHEOL, YOU ARE THERE. IF I RISE ON THE WINGS OF THE DAWN, IF I SETTLE ON THE FAR SIDE OF THE SEA, EVEN THERE, YOUR HAND WILL GUIDE ME, YOUR RIGHT HAND WILL HOLD ME FAST
(Psalm 139:7-10)

In a study of the attributes of God, one standing out would be His Omnipresence. This is the attribute of God telling us He is not limited or bound by space, He is present throughout all space. "Omni" is a prefix meaning "all". God is Omni ... All ... present totally. There is no place He is not.

Now, that's a concept worthy of meditation! Think of it! There is absolutely no place, anywhere, anytime, you can be where God is not present. He is there! Shouldn't this affect the things we do, the places we go? Knowing God is All-Present should be a source of great comfort, enhancing the confidence of daily living. Why? Because He is there! Yes, there are those times we may wander off the path, but that doesn't change His constant presence. He is always there, quick to lift up, anxious to answer your cry, ever present to wipe away a tear. He is there to rejoice with you when you happen to get it right. He is there to laugh with you when you find joy in His love.

Psalm 139:7-10 is a beautiful expression of God's Omnipresence. Here we see David realize his intensely personal relationship with the Lord cannot be limited by space.

And, you know what? Yours' isn't either! He is with you!

AN INSECURE CHRISTIAN? YOU'RE KIDDING!

If there is anything we face in this world, it's whether or not we are secure. Those who have been in long periods of unemployment know a little about the subject. Insecurity has lined the pocketbooks of many a psychiatrist.

Is being a Christian synonymous with being secure? Technically, and according to Scripture, yes. However, you and I know we can have a little breakdown in belief about the whole idea occasionally. Israel was very insecure after being in Egypt 400 years. Even after Moses was sent to deliver them, they were supplied with everything they needed. Their shoes lasted forty years (Every parents dream for their kids!), yet, they still couldn't trust God to take them into the Promised Land.   Insecurities surround us, and will not automatically go away. They must be faced with constant confession of who we are in Christ and what He has done for us. Instead of confessing what we can't do, say boldly;

"I CAN DO ALL THINGS THROUGH CHRIST WHO STRENGTHENS ME!"   (Phil.4:13)

Instead of confessing your weakness, remind yourself the Word says;
   "LET THE WEAK SAY, I AM STRONG!" (Joel 3:10)

Instead of confessing sickness, confess;
   "WITH HIS STRIPES I AM HEALED" (Isa.53:5)

Refuse to let your mouth violate your believing heart by uttering anything that defeats the finished work of the Lord Jesus on the Cross. Insecurity fades away as you realize your security is only found in Him.

In Jesus, you are a secure person!

TO PRAY IS TO CHANGE

MAKE ME TO KNOW THY WAYS, O LORD; TEACH ME THY PATHS. LEAD ME IN THY TRUTH AND TEACH ME. FOR THOU ART THE GOD OF MY SALVATION; FOR THEE I WAIT ALL THE DAY
(Psalm 25:4-5)

Psalm 25 contains a prayer that should be on our hearts as we press toward revival. Most prayers of the Bible are short, but effective. The Lord's Prayer consists of fifty-six words, yet, I recently read of a government order setting the price of cabbage that contained 26,911 words. Hmmm, some contrast, huh?

Allow me to share the following thoughts from "*Celebration of Discipline*", by Richard Foster:

"To pray is to change. Prayer is the central avenue God uses to transform us. If we are unwilling to change, we will abandon prayer as a noticeable characteristic of our lives. The more we pray, the more we come to the heartbeat of God. Prayer starts the communication process between ourselves and God. All the options of life fall before us. At that point, we will either forsake our prayer life and cease to grow, or we will pursue our prayer life and let Him change us. Either option is painful. To not grow in His likeness is to not enjoy His fullness. When this happens, a haunting voice continues to ask, 'What could I have become in Him if I would have been a man of prayer?' To grow in His likeness is to enjoy His fullness. When this happens, the priorities of the world begin to fade away."

Pray ... and enjoy the change!

DISCERNMENT ... FOR THE COMMON GOOD

TO EACH IS GIVEN THE MANIFESTATION OF THE SPIRIT FOR THE COMMON GOOD ...TO ANOTHER, THE DISCERNING OF SPIRITS.
(1 Corinthians 12:7,10)

To "discern", in this context, means you have the ability to discriminate, to separate thoroughly, to withdraw from a situation the reality not readily apparent to the casual observer. You can see the obvious like others, but also have insight into what isn't seen.

No, it's not ESP, it is a gift of the Holy Spirit. For example, in Acts 14:8-10, the Apostle Paul sees a man lame from birth ... it was obvious to all. Verse nine says Paul, *"Had seen that he had faith to be made well."* Paul discerned the man would respond to the Lord's provision of healing, which he did at Paul's command. If Paul hadn't acted on what he discerned to be true in the spiritual realm, the man would probably still be sitting there.

Sometimes, the gift of discernment is used in a negative fashion, pointing out problems in other people's lives. There may be a time for that, but the gifts are given *"for the common good."*

Use the gifts the Lord has given you to bring out the faith you know resides in those around you. Discern that spark in them that is just waiting for someone like you to say, *"Rise ... and walk!"*

MISSIONARY GRIT

"AS YOU GO, PREACH, SAYING, 'THE KINGDOM OF HEAVEN IS AT HAND'"
"BEHOLD, I SEND YOU OUT AS SHEEP IN THE MIDST OF WOLVES"
"AND YOU WILL BE HATED BY ALL ON ACCOUNT OF MY NAME"
"THEREFORE, DO NOT FEAR ..."
"AND HE WHO DOES NOT TAKE UP HIS CROSS AND FOLLOW ME, IS NOT WORTHY OF ME"
(Matthew 10:7,16,22,31,38)

It's been said, *"Christian missionary work is the most difficult thing in the world, it's surprising it was ever attempted."* (Stephen Neill) It is difficult, to say the least. But lest we be overcome by it's rigors, we must remember it is God's doing, not by our arm of flesh. God creates the missionary spirit. When He calls you (not if, when), He also places within you the necessary drive and strength to do it.

Some ingredients of the "Missionary spirit" are;

SPIRIT OF SACRIFICE: Who is going to give up a high paying job for a mission field? Many comforts may need to be set aside.

SPIRIT OF COURAGE: There is need of courage to face new experiences, some dangerous.

SPIRIT OF LOVE: This is the hallmark of the Christian faith. The motive of mission work must be love.

SPIRIT OF ZEAL: The term "Missionary", is synonymous with "zeal"

SPIRIT OF CONVICTION: There must be conviction that the Gospel of Jesus Christ is true, and people must hear it.

Sound impossible? It isn't ... you can do it, with Jesus. Allow your prayer life to impact your heart for missions, for that's the heartbeat of God. The world is starving for the life-giving Good News of Christ. The fields are white, ready for your participation.

Will you go?

HE LEFT SOMETHING BEHIND

AND STOOPING AND LOOKING IN, JOHN SAW THE LINEN WRAPPINGS LYING THERE, BUT HE DID NOT GO IN. SIMON PETER ALSO CAME FOLLOWING HIM, ENTERED THE TOMB, AND HE BEHELD THE LINEN WRAPPINGS LYING THERE
(Jn.20:5-6)

If someone was looking for you and they went to your closet, opened the door and looked in, what would they see? (I mean besides all that other stuff.) Would they find you there on a hanger, in your clothes? Well, barring a few rare cases, all that would be apparent would be empty clothes ... your "wrappings". One thing is sure, if the clothes are empty, you are not there!

Whatever the wrappings consisted of, the fact remains that Jesus left behind the "rags of death". They had a particular purpose ... to bind up one who is dead. Jesus had no need of such attire. He wasn't to be held by the tomb and some cloth wrappings, He was destined for Life! He came out of those rags, and out of the tomb! Those things would never hold Him again!

Resurrection Day is a good time to see if we still have any of the "wrapping" still clinging to us. Are there still some "rags" hanging on that covered the "old man"? We were all "dead in sin", wrapped about with the clothes of death, but Jesus set us free! He made us alive together with Him! We too, can emerge from the tomb, leaving behind the stained wrappings smelling of death. Leave them in the tomb and rise up in victory with the Resurrected One!

Don't be tempted to take them along, you won't be needing them ... the Lord has clothed us in His righteousness!

TO LIVE IS CHRIST ... TO DIE IS GAIN

She was eighty-five. Klara had slipped graciously through the veil we all long to see behind, but resist going there to see what it's like. She had lived a long life, experienced many joys, and grew stronger through her share of heartache and suffering. Sometime in her life, she came to know Jesus, and as her time drew near, she said to me, and others, I'm sure, *"I'm ready to go!"*

Through the stress and trial she must have suffered, she always had a smile. As cancer slowly drew the curtain, she would always have an encouraging word. While serving my week as Island Hospital Chaplain, I would anticipate visits with Klara as a blessing. In the midst of attempting to minister to so many people in pain, she would be a bright spot, an encouragement even in her affliction. She was a grand lady ... God must be pleased.

I TELL YOU THIS, MY BROTHERS; AN EARTHLY BODY MADE OF FLESH AND BLOOD CANNOT GET INTO GOD'S KINGDOM. THESE PERISHABLE BODIES OF OURS ARE NOT THE RIGHT KIND TO LIVE FOREVER ... FOR OUR EARTHLY BODIES, THE ONES WE HAVE NOW THAT CAN DIE, MUST BE TRANSFORMED INTO HEAVENLY BODIES THAT CANNOT PERISH, BUT WILL LIVE FOREVER.
(1 Corinthians 15:50,53)

I share this with you because we all must experience the ending of this life, as we know it. In spite of whatever mechanisms we use to block out the thought, it is reality. The Word of God, and personal experience, tell me the way I live now, the priorities and motives I choose, is going to have significant impact on the manner in which I step across the threshold.

What we see as death ... the end, God sees as life ... the beginning. Seems to me, we should look from His viewpoint, wouldn't you say? I'm thankful to Klara for reminding me God's grace is abundant right to the end, and the Presence of Jesus grows ever stronger.

Happy "Home-going", Klara! You've touched my life!

YOUR WORD IS GOOD

AND JOSHUA SAID TO THE PEOPLE, 'YOU ARE WITNESSES AGAINST YOURSELVES THAT YOU'VE CHOSEN FOR YOURSELVES THE LORD, TO SERVE HIM.' AND THEY SAID, 'WE ARE WITNESSES.'
(Joshua 24:24)

The Israelites made a decision at this point to turn from their foreign gods. They too, had been caught up in a "different gospel". By the words of their confession, Joshua made a covenant with them. They spoke their commitment and it was accepted as a signed contract.

Psalm 119:173 says, *"Let Thy hand be ready to help me, for I have chosen Thy precepts."*

The Psalmist is saying, *"Get ready God, here I come!"*

When we make a commitment, we know it. By the words of our mouth and the attitude of our heart, we choose God's precepts. What a joy to know His hand is ready to help. He will take us at our word, the word flowing from an honest heart. In our technical, business oriented society, there is much "red tape" requiring many signatures and countless copies of each form, yet, God still keeps His business refreshingly simple. He just says, *"Give me your word."*

Will you do it? Today?

LET'S HAVE A HEART SEIZURE!

AND WITHOUT FAITH IT IS IMPOSSIBLE TO PLEASE HIM, FOR HE WHO COMES TO GOD MUST BELIEVE THAT HE IS, AND THAT HE IS A REWARDER OF THOSE WHO SEEK HIM.
(Hebrews 11:6)

The German theologian, C.F.W. Walther, states;

"Faith is not the mere thought, 'I believe'. My whole heart must have become seized by the Gospel, and have come to rest in it. When that happens, I am transformed and cannot but love and serve God."

Dr. Walther made that statement in 1867; I believe it is still valid. How vital it is for us to have a "Heart Seizing" love for the Gospel and our relationship with Jesus! When God brings someone across our path with whom we can share the "Glad Tidings", we should pray they too will experience a "Heart Seizure". As the father of the demon-possessed boy cried, *"I do believe! Help my unbelief!"*

Let our own believing "Seize the Heart", that we may see the works of God in our midst! Today!

DEEPLY ROOTED

LISTEN TO COUNSEL AND ACCEPT DISCIPLINE, THAT YOU MAY BE WISE THE REST OF YOUR DAYS
(Proverbs 19:20)

"Superficiality is the curse of our age. The doctrine of instant satisfaction is a primary spiritual problem. The desperate need today is not for a greater number of intelligent people, or gifted people, but for deep people." (Richard Foster, 'Celebration of Discipline')

This is a truth worthy of consideration. It is fairly easy to exhibit many trappings of Christianity without actually listening to counsel and accepting discipline. To know Christ, and have stability in Him, these things must be a major part of your life. We are to seek and listen to wise counsel from God. Make an effort to learn to be disciplined in prayer and meditation, study of the Scriptures, worship, fasting, and service.

The times in which we live require the individual believer to be rooted in ever stronger, ever deeper soil. There is tremendous peace in really knowing, really having the assurance, that you are indeed deeply rooted in Christ."... *That you may be wise the rest of your days."*

TRANQUILITY, WHERE ART THOU?

FIRST OF ALL, THEN, I URGE THAT ENTREATIES AND PRAYERS, PETITIONS AND THANKSGIVINGS, BE MADE ON BEHALF OF ALL MEN, FOR KINGS AND ALL WHO ARE IN AUTHORITY, IN ORDER THAT WE MAY LEAD A TRANQUIL AND QUIET LIFE IN ALL GOODNESS AND DIGNITY.
(1 Timothy 2:1-2)

One of the reasons to pray for those in authority is that we might benefit. In God's order for the Believer, tranquility and quietness are definitely included. The stress from just plain daily living can be sufficient to prevent tranquility in any form. We are surrounded by noise and activity. Radios, everywhere you go only seem to work if they are vibrating with Rock music. Your perfectly normal children seem to go berserk when you least expect it. Your plans for retirement didn't include the freezer and the washing machine to go bankrupt at the same time. The teacher hands out a mid-term exam he announced while you were on an errand for him ... and he failed to mention it to you.

Tranquility? Quietness? Who has time for it? It seems none of us do. However, we all should. Times of meditation and solitude are vital to healthy Christian growth. Even in the middle of turmoil, there can be tranquility.

As the old hymn says, *"Like a river glorious, is God's perfect peace."*

It comes as we are *"Stayed upon Jehovah."*

MIRACLES!

HE CRIED OUT WITH A LOUD VOICE,"LAZARUS! COME FORTH!" HE WHO HAD DIED ... CAME FORTH!
(John 11:43)

MIRACLES!! ... "An event or action that apparently contradicts known scientific laws and is hence thought to be due to supernatural causes, especially an act of God." (Says Webster)

The Gospels list thirty-five separate "events" such as this, and many more are found throughout the Bible. Miracles continue to happen daily all over the world as God intervenes in the life of people.

Have you ever had a miracle? Do you know someone who has? If your answer is "No", I would suggest you look a little more carefully. We are usually looking for the stupendous, and missing the miniscule. A miracle is a miracle, regardless of the fanfare it may receive or not receive.

You experienced a miracle when Jesus made you a "new creation" in Christ. Every time you pray in the language of the Holy Spirit, you experience a miracle. Begin to look for miracles in every facet of daily living.

We have a God who tells us to *"Ask, and you will receive, that your joy be full."*

Expect God to work in miraculous ways as He shapes you into His image!

Are you ready for a miracle?

AH ... TO WORSHIP!

ASCRIBE TO THE LORD THE GLORY DUE HIS NAME
WORSHIP THE LORD IN HOLY ARRAY
(Psalm 29:2)

The Bible describes worship in physical terms. The root for the word, "Worship", is, "To prostrate". The word "Bless" literally means "To kneel" and "Thanksgiving", implies, "Extension of the hand".

Throughout Scripture, we find a variety of postures connected with worship. We see lying prostrate, standing, kneeling, clapping, lifting hands, dancing, lifting the head, bowing the head, wearing sackcloth and ashes, etc..

The posture of worship is connected to the Spirit of Praise. *"But, I'm the quiet, reserved type"*, we may say. (I've said it, haven't you?) Or, *"That's for the emotional fanatics."* (Those "other" people, right?)

We need to realize the question in worship is not, *"What will meet my need."* The question is, *"What kind of worship does God call for?"*

God desires wholehearted worship, and it's reasonable to expect it to be physical, as well as cerebral.

So, *"Ascribe to the Lord"!*

SPEAK IT!

DEATH AND LIFE ARE IN THE POWER OF THE TONGUE
(Proverbs 18:21)

YOU WILL DECREE A THING, AND IT WILL BE ESTABLISHED FOR YOU
(Job 22:28)

WE, HAVING THE SAME SPIRIT OF FAITH, ACCORDING TO WHAT IS WRITTEN, "I BELIEVED, THEREFORE I SPOKE", WE ALSO BELIEVE, THEREFORE WE ALSO SPEAK
(2Corinthians 4:13)

Hegge Iverson , founder of Burden Bearers, tells how his mother would exercise the truth of these and other Bible verses referring to the power of the tongue. By using this truth of Scripture, she was to see God perform many miraculous healings in her family and the salvation of her wicked husband.

If we are to do the works of God, we need to tap into this powerful means of restoration. It is not intended as a "gimmick", or as a "ministry" that is separate unto itself. This power, this exercising of faith, should be an integral part of the Spirit-filled life, a life based on a deep relationship with the Creator God,

The One ...

WHO GIVES LIFE TO THE DEAD AND CALLS INTO BEING THAT WHICH DOES NOT EXIST
(Romans 4:17)

Every time we pray for someone, we have an opportunity to stand on God's Word concerning this Truth.

Remember, it is God's will to use you! Today!

PENTECOST! PENTECOST!

AND SUDDENLY FROM HEAVEN CAME A NOISE LIKE A VIOLENT RUSHING WIND, AND IT FILLED THE WHOLE HOUSE WHERE THEY WERE SITTING. AND THERE APPEARED TO THEM TONGUES AS OF FIRE DISTRIBUTING THEMSELVES, ANDS THEY RESTED ON EACH ONE OF THEM. AND THEY WERE ALL FILLED WITH THE HOLY SPIRIT AND BEGAN TO SPEAK IN OTHER TONGUES, AS THE SPIRIT WAS GIVING THEM UTTERANCE

(Acts 2:2-4)

What can any one add to this powerful event that swept through the "Upper Room"? Nothing! It's only left for us to receive it ourselves!

The "normal" Christian walk should include the deep, flowing, throbbing Presence of the Holy Spirit ... the Comforter in times of trial; the Oil who keeps the Body of Christ working properly; the Fire who purifies; the Living Water who washes us and flows out to others; the Earnest on our inheritance; He is the Spirit of Holiness!

Be filled with the Holy Spirit!

HE IS OUR PEACE!

FOR HE HIMSELF IS OUR PEACE, WHO MADE BOTH GROUPS INTO ONE, AND BROKE DOWN THE BARRIER OF THE DIVIDING WALL
(Ephesians 2:14)

He is our peace ...praise God that it is He, not me, nor you, nor circumstances, whatever they may be. Most of us go through situations placing a real strain on our supply of peace. I, along with you, share in the same temptations. We will never, as long as we're in this world, be isolated from things that would pull and tear at us, trying to rob our peace. Why? Primarily because, *"The thief comes only to steal, and kill, and destroy ..."* (John 10:10a). Satan is just doing his job, and he can be very proficient at it.

However, the last part of John 10:10 says, *"...I came that they might have life, and that they might have it more abundantly."* God's peace is always available, never lacking in power, always abundant, and full of His grace and love.

It is common for us to lose peace when our focus strays from Jesus to "the problem". Each trial is an opportunity to experience His peace in the midst of the storm, when we choose to have our mind stayed on Him. How great is our God! How great is His peace!

IS ANYTHING TOO DIFFICULT?

THEN THE WORD OF THE LORD CAME TO JEREMIAH, SAYING, BEHOLD, I AM THE LORD, THE GOD OF FLESH; IS ANYTHING TOO DIFFICULT FOR ME?
(Jeremiah 32:26-27)

THE LORD SAID TO ABRAHAM ... IS ANYTHING TOO DIFFICULT FOR THE LORD?
(Genesis 18:14a)

Christians who make themselves available to God invariably seem to become involved in the needs of others. Some needs seem fairly trivial, except to the one in need. There are other situations so tragic and complex we can feel overwhelmed because we sense our own lack and apparent in-ability to help.

What do you think would happen if we could see these problems as Jesus sees them? Do you suppose some jobs are harder for God than others? Was it more difficult for Him to change the water into wine, or to raise the dead? Is it harder for Him to heal a case of the sniffles, or a case of cancer? Is it more of a strain on the Creator to bring your garden to harvest, or to set the moon and stars in place?

Do you ever feel your sin must surely be more difficult to forgive than sin someone else may have? Our perspective certainly has some effect on our faith, doesn't it? When Paul said, *"Let this mind be in you which was also in Christ Jesus"*, (Philippians 2:5) he was addressing humility, but this also impacts our perspective as well.

The "mind of Christ" says ...
"NOTHING IS TOO DIFFICULT FOR GOD!"

All jobs are easy for the Lord! Trust Him!

BE STEADFAST, IMMOVABLE

THEREFORE, MY BELOVED BRETHREN, BE STEADFAST, IMMOVABLE,
ALWAYS ABOUNDING IN THE WORK OF THE LORD, KNOWING THAT YOUR TOIL IS NOT IN VAIN IN THE LORD
(1 Corinthians 15:58)

"Therefore ..." Paul says. This verse follows his claim that *"Death is swallowed up in victory."* What a powerful truth!

Can we truly believe there is <u>nothing</u>, not even death itself, that can keep the Believer from victory in Christ?

I am so aware lately of our need to be steadfast in the Lord. Being steadfast in Jesus colors all we do and say. It makes a good mother or father a better mother or father. It causes us to be better citizens, better neighbors, better everything. Above all, it causes us to be better ambassadors for Jesus Christ.

I want to be a better witness for Christ, don't you? The Christian life is intended to be stable in spite of troubles or the negative influence of the world. *Lord Jesus ... help us to be steadfast.*

We are exhorted to *"abound in the work of the Lord."* What is the "work"? Have you ever asked yourself what work He has called you to? Are you "abounding" in it?. God's Word challenges us, doesn't it?

Know that your *"toil is not in vain in the Lord"*, and give thanks to God, who gives us victory through our Lord Jesus Christ!

Be steadfast ... Immovable.

PRAYER

Recently, my wonderful wife, Martha, brought home a book by Leonard Ravenhill, titled, *"Revival ... God's Way"*.

It is a book about the importance of prayer as it relates to revival. The Church is to be a praying Church if there is to be revival in our day, so the encouragement to prayer is an important one. Allow me to share the following thoughts from Mr. Ravenhill's book.

He says prayer is ....

The most unexplored area of the Christian life.

The most powerful weapon of the Christian life.

The most hell-feared battle in the Christian life.

The most secret device in the Christian life.

The most underestimated power in the Christian life.

The most untaught truth in the Christian life.

The most demanding exercise in the Christian life.

The most neglected responsibility in the Christian life.

The most conquering outreach in the Christian life.

The most warfare in the Christian life.

The most far reaching ministry in the Christian life.

Prayer is really the key to maturing in Christ. It is also the key to revival in our community.

Will you pray?

RIDE THE WIND

In Psalm 18:11 we find, *"...and He rode on a cherub and flew, and He appeared on the wings of the wind."*

One evening, Martha and I were up on Cap Sante, our local viewpoint, drinking in the grandeur as we're prone to do occasionally. There were many gulls in the air, and, as I watched, I realized they weren't doing much more than enjoying the ride on the updrafts flowing off the cliffs. There was such a lack of effort as they soared back and forth, never having to flap their wings until they slid away from the upward flow suspending them.

Of course, the spiritual parallel became pretty obvious as I enjoyed this feast to the eye. How like those gulls we need to be! Always riding on the breeze of the Holy Spirit ... only flapping our wings when we need to correct our course back into the continual updraft that is ever present, ever sustaining, with unlimited altitude ever available. It's that flowing not seen with the physical eye, but oh, how you can experience the Presence!

From time to time, I need to remind myself to quit thrashing the air and just relax on the flowing cushion of His Presence. It is in times such as this, when the intimacy the Holy Spirit is flowing around us, that we gain a fresh glimpse of what Isaiah meant when he wrote, *"They will mount up with wings as eagles ..."*

Stretch out your wings and relax.

A STAGNANT SPIRIT

In Zephaniah 1:12, God says, "...
I WILL SEARCH JERUSALEM WITH LAMPS, AND I WILL PUNISH THE MEN WHO ARE STAGNANT IN SPIRIT."

It also says these are men who say in their hearts, *"The Lord will not do good or evil."* They may not say as much, but they apparently don't believe God is very active in the affairs of mankind.

A stagnant spirit! How gross! I mean really; that has to be worse than a case of teen-age acne! Do you realize what characterizes something stagnant? King James, and others, use *"Settled on their lees"*, or, *"On their dregs"*, or, *"Sit contented in their sins"*. "Stagnant" is the word used in the New American Standard version, and I believe it's very descriptive. Something stagnant has no motion or current. It is not flowing and has become foul from the lack of movement. To prevent stagnation, something needs to be flowing in and something flowing out. (Just think of all the creepy crawlers living in a stagnant pool!) This is so descriptive of the life in Christ, isn't it? Anytime we feel stagnant, one of the first things to check would be the incoming flow, and the outgoing flow. If there is no flow, what do you have? Phew! Stagnant spirit! Stopping the refreshing flow leads to pretty dull Christianity ... not to mention the smell.

How's <u>your</u> flow? (sniff, sniff)

BELIEVE IN HIM

"Believe Me that I am in the Father, and the Father in Me; otherwise, believe on account of the works themselves. Truly, truly, I say to you, he who believes in Me, the works that I do shall he do also; and greater works than these shall he do; because I go to the Father. And whatever you ask in My name, that will I do, that the Father may be glorified in the Son. If you ask me anything in My name, I will do it."
(John 14:11-14)

    This Scripture is one having the ability to cause great rejoicing, or, can make us slink off with guilt and shame because our Christian walk may not be packed with signs and wonders.

    How many eyes have you opened this week? How many people have you led to Jesus today? You mean, you prayed for your kids, and they still act like kids? Did you raise anyone from the dead this week? Well ... what <u>have</u> you done?

    Lots of opportunity for guilt, isn't there? Don't be overcome by it. You see, Jesus said, "Believe ME ... Believe <u>in</u> ME." God's desire is that we see Jesus. The miraculous comes as HE is the object of worship, not the miracle.

    I earnestly desire to see miracles. I'm sure you do, also. However, we must not lose perspective in our earnestness. We have no reputation to defend ... We are not responsible for the success or failure of miracles. Our responsibility is to see Jesus ... Believe HIM ... Believe <u>in</u> HIM.

    He will honor His Word, for, *"Signs will follow those who believe"* ... and HE will be glorified!

FORGET IT!

DO NOT CALL TO MIND THE FORMER THINGS, OR PONDER THINGS OF THE PAST
(Isaiah 43:18)

These few words spoken by God to Israel, regarding their restoration, have the potential to completely change your life. Do you realize the relief available to you by taking God at His Word?

Everyone of us was locked in our sin until Jesus became our Lord. Some worked harder at it than others, but, *"we all sinned and fell short of the glory of God"*. It is one thing to be reminded of our sin by God ... He will do so that we may repent. However, He says, *"Don't call it to mind or ponder ..."*.

If you have confessed your sin and repented, it's gone! You don't have anything to ponder. Satan is the author of your past sins; he is the one who attempts to drive them into your mind so you will feel guilty and insecure and unclean. He is a liar! Those confessed sins are under the blood of Jesus! They are gone! Buried! Vanished! Washed away! Kaput! Don't call to mind those things which have been removed from your life. Instead, follow Paul's counsel in Philippians 4:8. *"If anything is worthy of praise, let your mind dwell on these things."*

There is always something worthy of praise. Always!

WE CAN REJOICE IN JESUS!!!

WE KNOW THAT ALL THINGS WORK TOGETHER FOR GOOD TO THEM THAT LOVE GOD, TO THEM THAT ARE CALLED ACCORDING TO HIS PURPOSE
(Romans 8:28)

IF GOD BE FOR US, WHO CAN BE AGAINST US?
(Romans 8:31)

     Hallelujah! Those two verses alone should fill the camp with joy! That's something to laugh about! We should laugh from pure joy! It's not necessary to have something to laugh at, something funny ... we can laugh because of the flow of joy that comes from knowing Jesus!
     A dear pastor friend in Idaho almost always laughs when someone gets healed in his services. It was an unexpected response at first, both to him and others, but that's what should happen! What a joyful occasion it is! We will always face many tests in life, but Jesus is our strength. We can be happy or miserable, it's our choice. Our attitude is what will show.
     If you are having a hard time showing a good, positive, happy attitude, learn to express solid Scripture based convictions, such as ...

- I CAN DO ALL THINGS THROUGH CHRIST WHO STRENGTHENS ME

- GREATER IS HE WHO IS IN ME THAN HE WHO IS IN THE WORLD

- IF GOD BE FOR ME, WHO CAN BE AGAINST ME?

- I CAN RUN THROUGH A TROOP AND LEAP OVER A WALL!

     Then ... expect your attitude to change. Turn up the corners of your mouth ... laugh instead of cry. God is your Father, Jesus is your elder brother --- now, that's something to be happy about!

YOU CAN TRUST HIM

WHEN I AM AFRAID, I WILL PUT MY TRUST IN THEE
(Psalm 56:3)

What a simple, yet profound truth! There was a young boy who watched his small kitten climb out on a small limb of an old tree. As it reached the end of the branch, it slipped and was hanging precariously by its front paws. (Like the poster that says, "Hang in there!") The boy knew he couldn't reach the kitten by climbing the tree because the branch wouldn't hold his weight. He tried to jump up and grab the branch but he was just too small to reach it. The boy realized the only way for the rescue was for the frightened kitten to fall into his arms.

He tried to coax it to let go, but the kitten just struggled frantically, trying to save itself. (Sound familiar?) Finally, it couldn't hold on any longer and fell ... right into the waiting arms.

Oh, how like that kitten we can be! We get out on a limb or into some scary situation, and make the wonderful discovery that God is there ... waiting for us to fall into His arms. He wants us to let go of all the things in which we place our trust, the things that so often let us down.

He wants us to trust in Him ... the One who never fails! Go ahead, let go!

DECIDE

CHOOSE THIS DAY WHOM YOU WILL SERVE
(Joshua 24:15)

John Adams, one of the staunch supporters of the Declaration of Independence, said,

"Sink or swim, live or die, survive or perish, I give my hand and my heart to this (Declaration). It may cost treasure and it may cost blood, but ... my whole heart is in it. All that I have and all that I am and all I hope in this life, I am now ready to stake upon it ... Independence now and Independence forever!"

The only way you can live a successful Christian life is when you reach a point where you decide you are going to serve God ... live or die, survive or perish, and, when you decide you are going to have faith God will take care of you, no matter what.

Our nation was founded on this kind of commitment. If there is that depth of allegiance to liberty, how much more should it be to Jesus Christ, the Author of Liberty and Independence?

"All to Him I owe ..."

LEARN THE LANGUAGE OF FAITH

Have you ever known someone who had no problems in their life? I haven't either!

It would seem problem solving is one of the major issues of life. Each day is filled with the need for decisions, each decision involving a problem of some sort. They can tend to be overwhelming, can't they? But, you know what? Each problem can be an opportunity to trust God. (Right here is where you say, *"Oh, sure!"*) It can be an opportunity to learn His ways, and experience in a very tangible way, His hand in your life.

Each problem overcome should result in an increase of our faith. Problems really should be faith-builders, not a pathway to discouragement and depression.

Part of the answer to the problems we face is in our language. As Paul says;

"For it is by believing in his heart that a man becomes right with God; and with his mouth he tells others of his faith, confirming his salvation." (Romans 10:10)

The words, the language, confirm his faith is valid. Continuous confession of faith in God's Word is the basis for the language of faith, a language that should be spoken daily. Practiced properly, in sincerity, it can bring about miraculous changes. It can lead others to commitment to Christ. It will develop your personal spiritual life. It can release God's power to bring forth miracles!

I realize there are many facets to this concept, some far-out and distorted, nevertheless, there is a proper place in a Believer's life to confess the positive Word of God and His ability to act in the midst of a very negative situation.

LET THE WORDS OF MY MOUTH AND THE MEDITATION OF MY HEART
BE ACCEPTABLE IN THY SIGHT, O LORD, MY ROCK AND MY REDEEMER. (Psalm 10:14)

"Acceptable words" are those releasing the power of God in your life as He uses you to tell others ... *"I love you ... I forgive you"*.

BURDEN BEARING

BEAR ONE ANOTHER'S BURDENS, AND THUS FULFILL THE LAW OF CHRIST
(Galatians 6:2)

FOR EACH ONE SHALL BEAR HIS OWN LOAD
(Galatians 6:5)

Does the Bible contradict itself? How can I bear someone else's burden when the Bible says to bear my own?

I realize this can become a "catch-all" scripture for those who want to justify worrying a lot. Do you know someone who always seems to be carrying the burdens of the whole world?

I believe what Paul is bringing out here, is the importance of being equipped to handle our own burdens. In this way, we will be available and able to help carry the load of others when called upon to do so. We all have a number of responsibilities, things unique to us and to no one else. Paul is telling us to learn to be strong in our own life, and then when the additional weight of another's need is placed upon us, we can carry their load as well.

It's not possible to effectively carry *"Else's"* load if we refuse, or haven't learned, to carry our own. The additional burden will be too much to bear. This is one reason why it is so important to grow in our Christian walk, to learn to know God.

Begin to do what the Bible says to do. Speak as the Bible says to speak. This is the spiritual relationship that builds good muscles. It will expand them beyond what is necessary for our own load, equipping us for the extra burden when it comes ... and it will.

BECOME USEABLE

FOR WE ARE HIS WORKMANSHIP, CREATED IN CHRIST JESUS FOR GOOD WORKS, WHICH GOD PREPARED BEFOREHAND, THAT WE SHOULD WALK IN THEM
(Ephesians 2:10)

Many times, in the years of repairing damaged automobiles, I've found it necessary to make various tools to do a specific job.

There were times when a special tool had to be fashioned. The tool may be used just that one time for the same need may never arise again. Usually, the tool was not designed to be especially attractive; looks were not that important. The important thing is, will it do the job? It's truly a *"Form follows function"* situation. When we think of being *"His workmanship"*, what thoughts form in your mind? Is the priority to be how you look or how you perform? The secular world places great emphasis on how you "look", and, as people living in this world, we tend to think the same way. Now, appearance is important, of course. How many of us go off to work or school looking like we were just dragged through a knothole? (One of my mother's favorite descriptions for me)

God created us as His tools, masterpieces fashioned to do His work in the lives of people. You may question Him at times, saying, *"God, why can't I be as pretty or handsome as that shiny tool over there?"* Experience has shown me the tools used most often are the ones that appear less attractive because they've had the "newness" worn off. The "newness" has been replaced with a polish only achieved from being used repeatedly by the Master Craftsman.

It is vitally important for Christians to have a healthy perspective of who we are and why we are. Priorities need to be re-evaluated consistently so we can be the tool God places in His hand, and yes, He will use you properly.

Become useable in the hand of the Craftsman.

RE-CREATION

Ah, summertime! The season of recreation and vacations! One of the blessings of living in this community is the availability of recreation year round. Not too many places have the beauty and possibilities found here. Many probably take it for granted, but when you are from wheat country or the desert areas of our country, this place is truly unique. Many people come here to recreate. The word "recreation", means "re-creation". A time set aside to re-create the mind and body, to become refreshed physically and mentally. This renewal time can be vital for effective performance on the job.

Isaiah gives a good formula for re-creation that doesn't involve money or a long journey with a car full of kids. (Does this interest you?)

He wrote; *"They that wait upon the Lord shall renew their strength; they shall run and not be weary; they shall walk and not faint."* (Isaiah 40:31)

It's possible to spend every cent we have by traveling to the most exotic spot in the world, and still come home with the same problems we thought would be left behind. Fact is, now that the pocket-book is empty, a new set of problems emerge. Usually, what is needed is not" recreation", but, "re-creation". A "re-creation" in the soul, a turning to God, remembering our sins are forgiven. Burdens and worries lift, hope is renewed and we truly become re-created in the whole person.

This truth is good to apply personally, but beyond that, as followers of Christ, we have many opportunities to share this with others. As we have contact with vacationing folks, look for ways to encourage them to be "re-created". We all see them in the supermarket, at the beach, in the shops, and at the marinas.

Place yourself in the "highways and byways", for that is where the people are who need someone to tell them ... "*You can run and not be weary, you can walk and not faint*" ... in Jesus.

EXPOSING THE ENEMY

Have you ever thought about the strategy Satan has used throughout history?

He tried to prevent the birth of the Messiah at Bethlehem. Failing at that, he tried to destroy and discredit Jesus, actually forcing events that ultimately brought Jesus to the cross, and just when the devil thought he had won ... he lost! Instead of removing Jesus from his sight, he had fulfilled the Word of God, burning the triumph of the cross into the heart of mankind! (Right about here you should shout, "Hallelujah"!)

Now it seems his tactics have changed slightly. Brother Andrew, of *"God's Smuggler"* fame, says;

"His attack is now two-pronged. Firstly, Satan now concentrates on the life and name of Jesus, which each believer bears as His representative. The attack you may be under is not just directed at you, but the life of Jesus in you, a life which you have the power to transmit to others."

Satan wants to discredit you and destroy your witness of new life to others. Brother Andrew goes on;

"The second prong is Satan's attack on the written Word of God."

Twisting Scripture has always been a favorite of his. Historically, he has used many means, including the Church, to prevent the printing and distribution of the Scriptures.

The Apostle Paul writes in Ephesians 5:11, *"Do not participate in the unfruitful deeds of darkness, but instead, even expose them."*

As believers in Jesus, it is our responsibility be aware of the enemy's tactics. Nurture and protect your relationship with Jesus Christ as though your life depends on it ... for it does! We are not to walk in fear. We are to know who we are in Christ. Knowing this sheds light on the darkness, exposing it for what it is.   We have the authority in Jesus Christ to have victory over Satan. There is great joy and liberty in living a holy life. God has given us the ability and opportunity to do so ... through the blood of Jesus Christ!

GO AHEAD ... LOVE YOURSELF

TEACHER, WHAT IS THE GREAT COMMANDMENT IN THE LAW? HE SAID TO HIM, "YOU SHALL LOVE THE LORD YOUR GOD WITH ALL YOUR HEART, AND WITH ALL YOUR SOUL, AND WITH ALL YOUR MIND ... THE SECOND IS LIKE IT, YOU SHALL LOVE YOUR NEIGHBOR AS YOURSELF."
(Matt.22:36-37,39)

I really appreciate it when people are clear and specific about a matter, don't you? Jesus was a clear communicator, and when He wanted to make a point, He did so. When the lawyer asked Him the question about the Law, Jesus didn't hedge or debate, He just laid it on the line. Instead of some legalistic works to be done, Jesus established Love as the greatest of all commandments.

What do you love? Jesus said there are three priorities;

- LOVE GOD: He is high above all, we are to worship only Him.

- LOVE YOUR NEIGHBOR: Who is your neighbor? It's much more than the person next door. Jesus said, "Love them."

- LOVE YOURSELF: This can be the most difficult.

Many people can't really love God or their neighbor because they have such self-hatred. Attitudes like, "Why am I this way", or, "I'll never amount to anything", or, "I just know everyone hates me", or any other accusations from Satan, point out the need for some self-love.

This is a delicate issue because we are not to be ego-centric or narcissistic, but we are to love and appreciate God's creation. If we belong to Jesus, then we are not our own, so love what is His. Does that make sense? You are precious in God's sight. He loves you so much He sent His only Son to establish a place for you. He thinks you are to be loved. Don't you think we should agree with God?

Love yourself ... it's okay!

SOWING GODLY SEED

Let's think about sowing for a moment. Sowing is a concept growing dim in our urbanized society. Children of today are rarely familiar with farm life. Sowing is an agricultural term meaning to plant or scatter seed for the purpose of growing a crop.

It is the purpose behind the sowing that is important. If we just threw seed on the ground and it never produced anything, we probably wouldn't do it again, would we? On the other hand, if we put out some seed, and gave it some care, even minimal attention, something would happen. There would be some production, some growth.

Scripture has some pointed things to say about sowing. Note Galatians 6:7-8;

DO NOT BE DECEIVED, GOD IS NOT MOCKED; FOR WHATEVER A MAN SOWS, THIS WILL HE ALSO REAP; FOR THE ONE WHO SOWS TO HIS OWN FLESH SHALL FROM THE FLESH REAP CORRUPTION, BUT THE ONE WHO SOWS TO THE SPIRIT SHALL FROM THE SPIRIT REAP ETERNAL LIFE.

What you sow, you reap. What you put in, you get out. This is a life principle established by God, and it works. Recently in our worship service, we dedicated a new-born child to the Lord. That's not an insignificant event. Part of that dedication challenged the rest of us to live faithfully for Christ, so that ... *"This child, and all other children in your midst, may grow up in the knowledge and love of Christ."*

We, as Christians, are to sow our lives into the lives of our children. We are to live Godly lives of integrity, giving the credit and glory to God, so that children will see an example of how to live righteously. Quite a responsibility, isn't it? If we sow Christlikeness, children have a definite opportunity to grow into Christlike adults. If we sow the world's standards, Christlikeness will be very difficult for them to comprehend or accept.

Let's scatter Godly seed, the harvest will be a joy!

THE PLACE OF BLESSING

HOW BLESSED IS THE MAN WHO HAS MADE THE LORD HIS TRUST, AND HAS NOT TURNED TO THE PROUD, NOR TO THOSE WHO LAPSE INTO FALSEHOOD
(Psalm 40:4)

This verse is one of many in the Psalms declaring the outcome of those who trust in God. It points out the fact we are presented with some options in life. We are offered the opportunity to hook up with the "Proud". The "Proud" could be an individual, or, a complete system of belief, refusing to accept God's plan for humanity. The Proud would say, *"I don't need God, I am my own god! Furthermore, if you come along with me, you can be your own god as well!"* Great ... as if we didn't have enough trouble already!

We are also offered the delightful choice of following after those who have "lapsed into falsehood". These would tell us there are treasures waiting in the shadows of the occult or other religions. There are tasty morsels of "truth" waiting to be devoured by those seeking acceptance or personal power. The Kingdom of Falsehood would say our trust should be in the Prince of Darkness instead of in the Prince of Peace. It would lead those who enter into the arena of fortune-telling, ESP, seances, astrology, false religions, tarot cards, drug and alcohol addiction, pornography, witchcraft, Dungeons and Dragons, etc.

All this falsehood is designed to lead people anywhere except to a relationship with Jesus Christ. The simple truth is ... there is blessing only in living for Jesus Christ. In living for Satan, there is only heartache and cursing. It cannot be both ways. We must choose the Kingdom we wish to inhabit ... and no, the borders do not overlap. *"How blessed is the man* (including women and children) *who has made the Lord his trust."*

Do you really want blessing in your life? Place your whole weight on Jesus ... that's trust.

CULTURE OR CHRISTIANITY?

An interesting series of events can be found in the fourth chapter of Luke's Gospel account.

- Notice ...
Vs.14: Jesus returned to Galilee in the power of the Spirit.
Vs.15: He began teaching in the Synagogues, and was praised by all.
Vs.22: And all were speaking well of Him;

- And then ...
Vs.28: And all in the Synagogue were filled with rage.
Vs.29: They rose up to cast Him out of the city and led Him to the brow of the hill on which the city had been built, in order to throw Him from the cliff.

So, there you are, just when things were going well! What happened between vs.22 and vs.28? How could the One who was so accepted and praised become so quickly reviled and persecuted?

Well, in that short passage of time, Jesus let them know who He was, what He came to do, and that even non-Jews were included in His agenda.

So much for pleasing the "Establishment". What is the application of this for us? We must be aware of the difference between our "Culture" and our "Christianity". The Jews reviled Jesus because they expected Him to be a feather in the hat of their cultural religion, one they had fashioned for their own convenience. Jesus poked a pin in their bubble because He chose to touch the downtrodden, the people who had been scorned and rejected.

We must never be afraid to ask ourselves, *"What would Jesus do?"* Oftentimes, the answer will cut across the grain of our American culture, as well as the fabric of many contemporary churches. It's not popular to stick up for the downtrodden.

But let's do it anyway ... Jesus would.

WEAKNESS = STRENGTH

GOD HAS CHOSEN THE WEAK THINGS OF THE WORLD TO SHAME THE STRONG.
(1 Corinthians 1:27)

FOR WHEN I AM WEAK, THEN I AM STRONG.
(2 Corinthians 12:10)

It's obvious our society places great stock in being strong. Physical fitness, athletics, diet, strong self-esteem, etc., are big business today. One has only to consider the myriad books, tapes, health clubs, etc., to see the emphasis we place on strength. To be weak in anything is considered very undesirable.

"Spiritual warfare" is a term implying a need for strength. To engage in battle, one must be strong. But, how can this be? The Bible says I should be weak, and if I'm weak, I'll surely lose the conflict. It seems we are faced with a dilemma, doesn't it?

Recently, I saw Corrie Ten Boom on a re-run of the 700 Club. It's always inspiring to hear this elderly saint recount the miracles of her confinement in Ravensbruck prison, a veritable suburb of hell. To me, she represents a classic example of the above Scriptures. Corrie knew her strength to not only survive, but help many others to do so as well, came totally from the Lord. She understood her physical weakness in no way hampered the ability of God's Holy Spirit to flow through her.

To be weak, in the New Testament context, is to realize salvation in the fullest sense of the word comes through trusting explicitly in the Lordship of Jesus, the One without whom we can do nothing. The key to victory in spiritual warfare is to lean on Jesus, not any strength we may perceive in ourselves.

What conflict are you facing? Whether it is emotional, physical, or spiritual ... your strength to overcome is dependent on your weakness, knowing God is in control. Make sense? Of course not! However, it is God's way ... and His way always works!

FOR INDEED, HE WAS CRUCIFIED BECAUSE OF WEAKNESS, YET HE LIVES BECAUSE OF THE POWER OF GOD. FOR WE ALSO ARE WEAK IN HIM, YET WE SHALL LIVE WITH HIM BECAUSE OF THE POWER OF GOD. (2 Corinthians 13:4)

IT'S TRUE! JESUS IS COMING!

WE DO NOT WANT YOU TO BE UNINFORMED, BRETHREN, ABOUT THOSE WHO ARE ASLEEP, THAT YOU MAY NOT GRIEVE, AS DO THE REST WHO HAVE NO HOPE.
(1 Thessalonians 4:13)

What is your ultimate hope? How far reaching is your concept of the future? As Christians, we have a glorious future poised on the other side of the veil between life on this earth and life in heaven.

If we truly believe Jesus died and rose again, then we must believe all who die in Christ will be raised to live eternally with Him. We who are alive when Jesus returns, will have to wait our turn, because those who have died will go first, then we will be taken. Don't worry though, it will happen so quickly we won't get bored, believe me!

The Lord is going to descend from Heaven with a shout. Apparently, MIchael the archangel, will be the one shouting, and the trumpet of God will be blown. Then, all the ones who believed and have died will burst forth from their resting places to be with the Lord. This will happen regardless of the condition of their body. Pretty amazing, isn't it?

After all this, (which probably doesn't take nearly as long as it does to read about it.) we who still live will be "caught up" (this is where we get the word, "Rapture") together with them in the clouds to meet the Lord in the air. And ... we will always be with the Lord!

What you have just read is a brief paraphrase of 1st. Thessalonians 4:13-17. I believe it is a crucial time for all Followers of Christ, for our world is rapidly moving into a mode of immoral, insane behavior. As Christians, we must remember our hope is found only in a personal relationship with Jesus Christ, not in any world system.

So, what is the Good News? Jesus is coming! The above passage ends with verse eighteen saying, *"Therefore, comfort one another with these words".*

So, be comforted, loved ones, Jesus is on the horizon! A great future awaits all who call on His name!

KEEPING PERSPECTIVE

Reminding the believers at Corinth of God's goodness, Paul writes;

I THINK YOU OUGHT TO KNOW, BRETHREN, ABOUT THE HARD TIME WE HAD IN ASIA. WE WERE REALLY CRUSHED AND OVERWHELMED, AND FEARED WE NEVER LIVE THROUGH IT. WE FELT WE WERE DOOMED TO DIE, AND SAW HOW POWERLESS WE WERE TO HELP OURSELVES;BUT THAT WAS GOOD, FOR THEN WE PUT EVERYTHING INTO THE HANDS OF GOD, WHO ALONE COULD SAVE US, FOR HE CAN EVEN RAISE THE DEAD.
(2 Corinthians 1:8-9 LB)

Paul's experience points us to two facts ....

1. He knew he was powerless to help himself.
2. He recognized God alone could save him.

Another important aspect is Paul's perspective of the situation. He realized his dependence on God was a good thing, not a bad thing. It wasn't a sign of weakness, rather, it was an indication of strength, strength of character and faith arrived at through relationship and service in Christ.

Are you being a "Do-it-yourselfer"? Our society is geared that way. It's difficult to be American and be dependent at the same time. It must be in our genes or something. We so easily take on the attitude of being our own boss, doing our own thing, and if God wants to come along and bless our endeavor, fine. It's, *"C'mon God, pull, push, or get out of the way!"* Quite a contrast to Paul's crisis, isn't it?

In a newsletter of Skagit Crisis Pregnancy Center, I read this tidbit of wisdom;
"Two Foundation Facts of Human Enlightenment: There is a God ... You are not Him."

Give it some thought ... place your whole weight on Jesus. (Both feet!)

JESUS WASN'T A "CLOSET CHRISTIAN"

AND I KNOW THOU HEAREST ME ALWAYS; BUT BECAUSE OF THE PEOPLE STANDING AROUND I SAID IT, THAT THEY MAY BELIEVE THOU DIDST SEND ME
(John 11:42)

And then, "He cried out with a loud voice, 'Lazarus! Come forth!'" And he did! Lazarus came back to life and they unwrapped the burial clothes from him!

What do think would have happened if Jesus had decided to be a "Closet Christian"? I know it sounds ridiculous, but suppose Jesus just allowed His relationship with the Father be known among those of like mind. Only the "12" were to know He was "religious". Who He was on the "street" wouldn't reflect His Messiahship, after all, He didn't want to be embarrassed. He would want to fit in with "The Guys".

Pretty tough to see Jesus like that, isn't it? Rightly so, for He was definitely the opposite. He was forthright and public about all He did. As I see it, the Bible builds a pretty strong case we should be the same way.

How are you doing? Are you confessing Jesus before others? Do those around you, especially your family members, know where you stand with Christ? Is your lifestyle being continually reshaped into His likeness? When we commit to Jesus, the changes He brings about are obvious and impossible to hide, unless we choose to suppress them. If we muffle and hush up those adjustments He is making, our relationship with Him dwindles until it becomes non-existent. Let's not be a "Closet Christian". There are many more Lazarus' out there who need to be raised from the dead. And yes ... you can do it.

Let's pray about it, alright?

FATHER, I REPENT FROM TRYING TO BE A CHRISTIAN JUST WHEN IT'S CONVENIENT OR NON-THREATENING. I WANT TO BE AN "ON-FIRE" CHRISTIAN ALL THE TIME. FILL ME WITH YOUR HOLY SPIRIT AND REMIND ME TO GLORIFY YOU, AND ONLY YOU, IN EVERY AREA OF MY LIFE ... IN JESUS' NAME! AMEN!

Amen?

BE FREE ... HONESTLY!

IF THEREFORE THE SON SHALL MAKE YOU FREE, YOU SHALL BE FREE INDEED.
(John 8:36)

What does it really mean to be "Free"? In the context of the above Scripture, it specifically means Jesus, the Son of God, frees us from the dominion of sin.

As Paul writes in Romans 6:14, "*Sin shall not be master over you.*" Webster has a lot to say defining "*free*", but it boils down to being "*set loose from any sort of entanglement or restraint.*"

Being free doesn't mean there are no rules or guidelines. True freedom is only maintained in an atmosphere of discipline and submission in Christ, otherwise there is only anarchy. God wants people free. Satan wants people bound. It's really that simple, and that's the battleground for the committed Christian.

A "Freeing" came for me one night in 1968. I was a pretty new Christian and the Lord had begun to convict me about smoking. Like most, I had tried some half-hearted attempts at quitting, to no avail. Freedom came one night when I rolled out of bed, got on my knees before Jesus, and confessed to Him I really didn't want to quit, I enjoyed smoking. That's when He set me free! I had smoked steadily for fifteen years and He totally released me! No withdrawal or struggle ... none! Just Free!

So, how did it happen? I don't have all the answers to that experience, but one thing I do know ... I finally "came clean" with God. There is something about honesty and integrity that pleases God. I've seen it in too many instances to discount it.

Are you bound by something? Do you really want to be free, or is it a piece of security for you? Being set free can be a little threatening at times. It means stepping out in faith, trusting in Jesus instead of Budweiser, or cocaine, or a cult, or anything else. It can mean earning to live life in a completely different environment, one of trust and submission to the Lordship of Jesus Christ.

Kinda scary, huh? But, do you know what? You can do it! Jesus will set you free! Amen?

Let's pray about it, right now....

God, I know I need to be free, but I can't seem to let go of this thing that has become so ingrained in my life. I know it is harmful to me, yet if I don't have it, I don't know what can fill that void.

I know true freedom is only in Jesus, so please come into my life and set me free from everything keeping me bound. I renounce it in the name of Jesus Christ, for the Bible says,

"He whom the Son sets free, is free indeed."
(John 8:36)

In the powerful name of Jesus Christ, The Liberator!

BEING FAITHFUL

MANY A MAN PROCLAIMS HIS OWN LOYALTY, BUT WHO CAN FIND A TRUSTWORTHY MAN?
(Proverbs 20:6)

This Scripture poses an interesting and challenging question. It is saying, *"Many will say they are loyal to the end, but it is difficult to find someone who will be faithful through thick and thin."*

I'm reminded of Peter, who so proudly and publicly said he was ready to go to prison and even die for the cause of Christ, (Lk.22:33) but quickly denied Him when the chips were down.

The Bible abundantly reveals God's faithfulness to His people. However, it also speaks very pointedly to our responsibility to be faithful as well. That's not always comfortable because it requires something of us ... a commitment to "be there".

In the Parable of the Talents, (Matt.25:14-30) Jesus established a profound spiritual truth easily applied in a practical manner. He said if we are faithful in small things, we can be trusted in larger things. I often use this truth to help establish various ministries within our church. If someone new comes, saying they want to provide some type of ministry, my reply is, *"Come, spend some time in worship with us, then we'll see."*

I find it is a rare person who is willing to be faithful instead of just wanting to do "their thing". Most will leave, looking for an arena where accountability and faithfulness aren't really required.

Loved ones, I firmly believe it is God's heart for us to be faithful, don't you? Faithful to Jesus. Faithful to family. Faithful to each other. Faithful to the Church. To be faithful means there are times we must forego personal comfort and convenience. It demands a servant's heart, and at times, causes us to question our sanity.

However, God will bless it, as Proverbs 28:20 says;
"A faithful man will abound with blessings ..."

Be faithful ... Be blessed!

YOU ARE A SHRINE

DO YOU NOT KNOW YOU ARE A TEMPLE OF GOD, AND THAT THE SPIRIT OF GOD DWELLS IN YOU? IF ANY MAN DESTROYS THE TEMPLE OF GOD, GOD WILL DESTROY HIM, FOR THE TEMPLE OF GOD IS HOLY, AND THAT IS WHAT YOU ARE.
(1 Corinthians 3:16-17)

This very plain and specific word was presented to the church at Corinth by the apostle, Paul. They needed to be reminded of the sacredness of their relationship with Christ. So do we.

We are His "Temple", individually and corporately. "Temple", in this context, describes something containing an object of worship. It literally means, *"Shrine or Sanctuary."*

For the pagans of the day, it was the place housing their idols. Paul expands the word to be that which contains the presence of God's Spirit, a Sanctuary, a dwelling place of the Holy Spirit.

As a Believer, can you see yourself in that context? Can you agree with the Word of God concerning who you are? We must note the warning attending this, as well. We are told the temple must not be destroyed. If we do destroy it, judgment happens. Kinda heavy, isn't it?

How do we apply something like this? To simplify to the extreme, it is saying...

- As a Believer, I must regard myself as holy property. I should do whatever is necessary to keep this "Shrine" in good repair. I am not to worship the Temple, I am to worship the One dwelling therein.

- As a Church, we are to treat the building, the implements of worship, and especially the people, with a sense of sacredness. Not because they are of value in themselves, but they are dedicated to the Lord Jesus Christ, the One who's Spirit dwells within His people, the Church. We should not allow anything or anyone to destroy what is set apart for God.

This Scripture can affect us at least two ways;

We can be arrogant and prideful in the knowledge God has chosen to live in His people,

or,

We can be humbled and repentant, realizing and embracing the tremendous grace exhibited to us by such a loving God.

I think we should opt for the latter, don't you?

STAY IN THE LIGHT

The second chapter of Isaiah begins with his prophecy of some good things on the horizon for Israel. However, the promise for the bright future would depend on their response to Isaiah's message in verse five, where he exhorts...

COME, HOUSE OF JACOB, AND LET US WALK IN THE LIGHT OF THE LORD.

This is really a very foundational truth. In essence, he is saying;

"If you walk in the light, you receive blessing. If you walk in darkness, you will experience grave consequences."

This truth is repeated in the New Testament.
1 John 1:7, tells us;

IF WE WALK IN THE LIGHT AS HE HIMSELF IS IN THE LIGHT, WE HAVE FELLOWSHIP WITH ONE ANOTHER, AND THE BLOOD OF JESUS HIS SON CLEANSES US FROM ALL SIN.

A breach of fellowship affects more than the one who chooses to play around in the dark. As Christians, we are learning to love one another, so when someone wanders off, it affects the whole Body. How do you feel when a brother or sister in the Lord decides to slide back into the muck? There's a pain in the heart, isn't there?
Sin in others causes the whole Body to hurt. Nobody sins alone. Let's break bread together, walking in the Light.

PRAYER IS NO JOKE

How's your prayer life? What's that? You wish I wouldn't ask? If that's what you're thinking, you're not alone.

I face the same obstacles you do when it comes to prayer. There's never enough time, I'm too busy, Whoops! There goes the phone, the lawn needs mowing, I'm late for the meeting, and on and on ... right?

I would like us to understand, regardless of barriers thrown up before us, we are going to pray! Will you agree to that?

Following Paul's exhortation to put on the armor of God, he says,

"With all prayer and petition, pray at all times in the Spirit." (Ephesians 6:18)"

Pray", he said. *PRAY!* Satan will try to convince us it doesn't matter if we pray or not. *"Whatever will be, will be"*, he says. That's not so! Whatever will be will be what we pray according to God's will in the powerful name of the Risen Christ ... the name of Jesus!

It's not uncommon to hear someone say, *"I'll pray about it."* Somehow, it never happens, not really. Oh, it is well meant, but the subtle working of Satan prevents it from actually taking place. Know what I mean? We end up talking it to death, but never pray about the matter.

People who pray are a direct threat to the kingdom of darkness, did you know that? Did you know you have the potential to change the course of circumstances? If you are a Born-Again Follower of the Lord Jesus Christ, filled with His Holy Spirit, you are a powerful, useable, anointed, justified, sanctified vessel fit for the Master's use!

Will you let Him use you? Pray! It's no joke!

THE POWERFUL ENTRY

AND SUDDENLY THERE CAME FROM HEAVEN A NOISE LIKE A VIOLENT RUSHING WIND, AND IT FILLED THE WHOLE HOUSE WHERE THEY WERE SITTING
(Acts 2:2)

So began the miraculous outpouring of God's Holy Spirit on earth. I find it interesting and invigorating, that He didn't creep in silently and subtlety in some obscure place.

Wasn't it great! God said to the Spirit, *"Go for it!"* (Well, maybe not those exact words) The Holy Spirit came exploding into the room! Nothing quiet, nothing nice and tidy, nothing sophisticated, just the awesome power of God charging in to take up residence in the hearts of His people. Flames of fire appeared over their heads, they began to speak with other tongues, and the burning power of Christ began to throb within each breast! Men and women touched by the Hurricane of Heaven never to be the same, and who would become a world shattering force!

Wouldn't you have loved to be there? Me too! Do we dare to believe the same thing is possible today? In a word, YES! Oh, we may never be in Jerusalem, the circumstances may be different, we may not see flames of fire (but don't rule it out) but ... BUT ... the same Holy Spirit will come crashing into your life as well, if you let Him. That's right; you must make the invitation, and allow Him access when He comes. If you send out the invitation, He will show up at your door! Remember, those folks in the Upper Room (120 of them) had been spending a lot of time together in prayer, obeying the command of Jesus to wait for this event to take place ... and it did!

How about you? Have you received the Holy Spirit since you believed? If you aren't sure, you need to settle the issue. If you haven't received Him, your Christian walk is lacking a major component. Do you really want to be part of a "Spirit-filled" church?

The only way for that to happen is for YOU to be filled with His Spirit. Amen?

I HOPE SO

Hebrews 11:1 tells us,
"Faith is the assurance of things hoped for."

What are you hoping for?" Hope" is an interesting word, isn't it? In the New Testament it is commonly translated as "Trust". To hope is to trust. However, my observation of hope is usually tinged with an element of "Un-hope".

Let me explain. I will ask someone, *"Are you going to heaven?"* The usual reply is, *"I hope so."* I ask, *"Do you believe Jesus will heal you?"* The usual reply, *"I hope so?"* I ask, *"Do you believe God loves you?"* The reply, *"I hope so."*

This response of *"I hope so"*, in most instances, is not usually filled with faith. The meaning of "Hope" then becomes, *"I'm really not sure, I really don't know, but it would be great and I would feel wonderful if it is true."*

In other words, *"I hope so"* becomes a statement of doubt rather than a confident trust in the ability and desire of God to accomplish His will in our life.

So, again I ask you ... what are you hoping for? Whatever it is, check it out with the Word of God to see if it's in His will. (Yes, you can know God's will) If it is, then trust Him completely.

Next time you are faced with a question prompting a reply of, *"I hope so"*, answer with a bold, *"Yes, I have hope for this because I trust God to do it, and do it with excellence!"*

NOW, MAY THE GOD OF HOPE FILL YOU WITH ALL JOY AND PEACE IN BELIEVING, THAT YOU MAY ABOUND IN HOPE, BY THE POWER OF THE HOLY SPIRIT.
(Romans 15:13)

THE MARK OF A CHRISTIAN

What should be the identifying mark of a Christian? If someone would stop you on the street and ask, "Do you know God?", what would be your reply?

Challenging questions. Questions for which we need an answer. I'm convinced Satan's priority is to convince people God cannot be known. But, He <u>can</u> be known! He <u>wants</u> us to know Him! How can we know God? What is a "litmus test" able to satisfy my desire to know Him?

I believe John 4:7-8 serves well, as it tells us;

BELOVED, LET US LOVE ONE ANOTHER, FOR LOVE IS FROM GOD, AND EVERYONE WHO LOVES IS BORN OF GOD AND KNOWS GOD. THE ONE WHO DOES NOT LOVE DOES NOT KNOW GOD, FOR GOD IS LOVE.

Let's do that again from the Living Bible ---

DEAR FRIENDS, LET US PRACTICE LOVING EACH OTHER, FOR LOVE COMES FROM GOD, AND THOSE WHO ARE LOVING AND KIND SHOW THEY ARE THE CHILDREN OF GOD, AND THAT THEY ARE GETTING TO KNOW HIM BETTER. BUT, IF A PERSON ISN'T LOVING AND KIND, IT SHOWS HE DOESN'T KNOW GOD, FOR GOD IS LOVE.

Quite a challenge, isn't it? According to the Lord, the bottom line is <u>love</u>. Signs and wonders, goose bumps, gifts of the Spirit, and various "feelings", may all be happening and can be wonderful, but if there is no love, it's just so much noise, a "clanging cymbal".

The early Church stood out in their culture because of their love. Love for Jesus and love for the brethren. Love is the "numero uno" commandment ... *"Love God with all your heart ... and your neighbor as yourself."*

We may say, *"Okay, I'm convinced I'm supposed to love, but how do I do it?"* The initial thought is of something to "do" for someone. That's alright, but my counsel is to learn to love God first. Love must flow from our love for Him. Do you honestly seek God? Do you read His Word? Do you really pray? Do you fellowship with His people, whether you like them or not? Are you reaching out to those who don't know Jesus with an attitude of love? God has called us to love! We must not allow pettiness or self-interest to overshadow the mandate of the Lord. *KEEP YOURSELF IN THE LOVE OF GOD.(Jude 21)*

GO AHEAD ... BE HAPPY

HOW HAPPY ARE THE PEOPLE WHOSE GOD IS THE LORD
(Psalm 144:15b)

It's O.K. to be happy. Did you know that? There are many things about our world that are not great occasions of joy, however, happiness for the Christian is founded on a different source. One not of this world. Our happiness flows from a relationship with our Creator. A catchy tune of recent date tells us, *"Don't worry ... Be happy!"* Good advice, isn't it? Happiness puts a smile on our face, and I know that pleases the Lord. I recently read somewhere, *"A smile is the light in the window of your face that tells people your heart is at home."*

Radio, T.V., magazine ads, and billboards, tell us happiness is found in various products. If we will just eat or drink or smoke their product, or travel to their chosen vacation spot ... we will be <u>so</u> happy! Many people respond to this hype because they desperately want to be happy. If I would do all the media says, I would end up broke, a physical wreck, and not at all happy.

The Hebrew word for "Happy", is "Esher", meaning, *"To be straight, level, honest, proper."* The New Testament word is "Makarios", defined as, *"Supremely blessed, fortunate."* From this, we can glean a meaning of Happiness. As we are honest with God, we will be supremely blessed. Blessings, i.e., happiness, flows to us from God. He makes us happy for He is our happiness. Before I knew Jesus, I too sought happiness in the "waste places". I never found it until I let Jesus take my arm in His, as He said, "Let's do this together."

"Now, I'm happy! Are you?

PETER

SHE RAN AND CAME TO SIMON PETER ... PETER, THEREFORE, WENT FORTH ... SIMON PETER CAME ... AND ENTERED THE TOMB
(John 20:2,3,6)

Easter Sunday is Resurrection Day. Actually, every Sunday is Resurrection Day, but Easter Sunday is the special time we celebrate our Risen Savior. He was crucified, placed in a tomb and sealed off, but not even death could restrain our Victorious Christ! Hallelujah!

In the midst of this great miracle, we see a man charging about, attempting to grasp the meaning of it all. Peter, the brash fisherman. Peter was outspoken and quick to confront when he thought it necessary. He was bold in his walk with Jesus. He was bold to declare Jesus as, *"The Christ, the Son of the Living God!"* (Matthew 16:16)

He was even bold that fateful night when he said, *"I do not know The Man!"* (Matthew 26:72) Through Peter, we can see the "humanness" of a relationship with Jesus. I'm impressed with the fact Peter ran right past John at the tomb entrance. While John stopped to "scope things out", Peter just charged right in. Not giving it a thought, he boldly invaded the place of death, because he knew it was where his source of life had been placed. The fact Jesus was no longer there was immaterial, Peter had a heart to love Jesus. He was deeply repentant he had denied Jesus and would go to any length to restore that kinship.

I'm glad the saga of Peter has a happy ending, aren't you? Jesus allowed the opportunity for Peter to receive his forgiveness and peace. The Book of Acts adequately reveals the good fruit borne in Peter's life, a fruit of repentance.

Can you relate to Peter? I sure can. We too, can be quick to publicly broadcast Jesus, then deny Him by serving "Self" instead of Him. We also make mistakes, as did Peter. However, let's learn from him; if our hearts are sold out to serve the Master, the Master will walk with us through all circumstances of life. ALL! The One who was crucified now lives! It's real! Not a myth nor a fable... IT IS REAL! Happy Resurrection Day!

GREATNESS

Did you ever entertain thoughts about being "great"? As a child, many dreams flow through the mind. There are aspirations to be a pilot, a star athlete, a race car driver, a beautiful model, a cowboy, a fireman or policeman, a mountain climber, a salesman (salesman?), etc.

Funny how things go, isn't it? As a kid, I would spend hours practicing jiu-jitsu and gymnastics on an old mattress in the back yard. It must have been quite a spectacle for the neighbors. How did I know I would become a pastor? God amazes me.

What were your dreams? What have you done with them? It's not too late, you, know. The idea of being too old is baloney, don't let that be an issue. But what does it really take to be great? To find the answer, we must look to Jesus.

Matthew 18:1-6 tells us;

THE DISCIPLES CAME TO JESUS, SAYING, WHO THEN IS GREATEST IN THE KINGDOM OF HEAVEN? AND HE CALLED A CHILD TO HIMSELF AND SET HIM BEFORE THEM, AND SAID, TRULY I SAY TO YOU, UNLESS YOU ARE CONVERTED AND BECOME LIKE CHILDREN, YOU SHALL NOT ENTER THE KINGDOM OF HEAVEN. WHOEVER HUMBLES HIMSELF AS THIS CHILD, HE IS GREATEST IN THE KINGDOM OF HEAVEN. AND WHOEVER RECEIVES ONE SUCH CHILD IN MY NAME, RECEIVES ME; BUT WHOEVER CAUSES ONE OF THESE LITTLE ONES TO STUMBLE, IT IS BETTER FOR HIM THAT A MILLSTONE BE HUNG AROUND HIS NECK AND HE BE DROWNED IN THE DEPTH OF THE SEA.

Sounds like Jesus is pretty serious about this, huh? So how do we become great? Become converted: Repent. Cut off the old, become new. Become childlike: not childish. Be openly honest with God. Humble yourself: Agree with Jesus that you are nothing without Him. Love other children: Be a stepping stone, not a stumbling block.

Greatness such as this won't earn you many points with your old "friends", but it goes a long way with God.

You <u>can</u> be great in God's Kingdom.

RESIST THE THIEF

THE THIEF COMES ONLY TO STEAL, KILL, AND DESTROY; I CAME THAT THEY MIGHT HAVE LIFE, AND THAT MORE ABUNDANTLY
(John 10:10)

Thieves can come in a multitude of shapes and sizes. What thief is prying at your window? Jesus came to pluck the thief off your windowsill and destroy his works. He desires abundant life for you. He wants all the locks and bolts off the windows. He desires them to be thrown open wide so the fresh wind of His Spirit can blow through with refreshing purity, making all the musty corners smell good.

Satan wants you to nail all your doors and windows tightly shut, to close the curtains, turn off the lights, and then sit in a corner while mold takes over. God wants <u>good</u> for His kids! Healing is part of the Abundant Life!
- Healing of the sick or broken body
- Healing of attitudes
- Healing of relationships
- Healing of a broken heart
- Healing of a troubled spirit.

God's desire is Wholeness and Wellness for body and soul. Will you relax your grip on pride and "self"? Will you encourage His access to your innermost being? Will you allow Him to heal you?

It's okay, you can trust Him.

TRADITIONAL VALUES

"*Tradition!*", declares Tevye in *"Fiddler on the Roof"*. In this story of Jewish hardship, (one of my favorites) we see the main character, Tevye, resist changes confronting his concept of what is right, or "traditional". From his perspective, "Tradition" equals "Correctness," not always a proper or popular stance. However, tradition also speaks of steadfastness, faithfulness to what we have come to accept as true and good.

I've recently read the biography of General Colin Powell, former Chairman of the Joint Chiefs of Staff. In this account, I'm once again reminded that some traditional values are of utmost importance. Gen. Powell's rise to his position of international influence can be traced to "traditional values", e.g., a strong sense of family loyalty, education, hard work, commitment to Christ, faithfulness in his marriage, love of country, and a heart to serve. He is a major contributor to society because of who he is as a person.

My encouragement to you would be this: Don't hesitate to exercise "traditional values". We must remember there is a solid foundation of tradition based on Scripture that produces steadfast living. It's okay to tell your kids "No" (and ""Yes", as well). It's okay to love your own spouse. It's okay to work hard. It's okay to love God and country. It's okay to learn as much as you can. It's okay to be faithful in Church attendance. It's okay to vote and be involved in politics. It's okay to be nice.

This line of thought leads me to a few verses worth remembering;
In 2 Thessalonians 3:3 & 5, Paul writes ...

BUT THE LORD IS FAITHFUL, AND HE WILL STRENGTHEN AND PROTECT YOU FROM THE EVIL ONE

Live for the Lord, He will take care of you!
MAY THE LORD DIRECT YOUR HEARTS INTO THE LOVE OF GOD AND INTO THE STEADFASTNESS OF CHRIST

It's okay to Live For Jesus!

RUN WITH THE HORSES!

If you have run with footmen and they have tired you out, then how can you compete with horses? If you fall down in a land of peace, how will you do in the thicket of Jordan?
(Jeremiah 12:5)

The thought here is that Jeremiah has found it difficult to deal with those "in the thicket", the ones who give lip service to God but have their mind, i.e., their intentions, motives, attitudes, desires, etc., far from the reality of a commitment, a submission to the King of kings. God is saying to Jeremiah that his own people will be more difficult for him to deal with than the heathen. He will find it hard in the places where he would expect comfort. He will discover trial and opposition where he would expect reception of his message and cause.

Isn't this the case with those who truly desire to serve Christ? I've found the message of servanthood to be one to which people will give mental assent, however there is a reluctance to accept what is perceived by some to be a lack of power. I've come to believe the real position of power with God is the place of servanthood. There is authority in Christ through being in submission to His way, not my own.

Early in my Christian walk, the words of Dietrich Bonhoeffer, *"When Christ calls a man, he bids him come and die"*, was a thought that began to direct my thoughts in being a disciple of Jesus. Sharing this message with others is often met with some reservation. It's a hard message, yet, according to my understanding of Jesus, it's the way he came, the way He walked, and the way He departed.

It seems to me to be the way He desires me to live. I find it very uncomfortable at times, yet I'm positive it's the way of Christ.

2 Corinthians 5:17, says, *"If any man is in Christ, he is a new creation; the old has passed away, behold, the new has come."* For the Christian, it must be assumed that there has been a spiritual death; the old man has died and is now renewed, resurrected, and in Christ. That's the foundation of water baptism. Without the spiritual "death" of the old person; repentance is the word, a new person cannot emerge.

To *"run with the horses"*, I must be a dead man. To the "world", it's an illogical concept. The world's perspective would be that if one is to run with the horses, there must be power released. They would say only power can conquer; only power is able to keep up with those who travel in the "fast lane". Scripture teaches just the opposite. True power, true authority, flows from a relationship with the One who gave Himself completely.

Those who would be victorious, must be dead to the old nature. Jesus said that He came to serve, not to be served. Seems to me He knew what He was doing.

So, would you like to run?

Finally, and most importantly ------------

If you've never found a place of peace in your life, it's nearer than you might imagine. Jesus Christ was nailed to a cross for our sins, yours and mine.
As bad as things may seem, nothing is beyond the reach of God's forgiveness available in Jesus Christ. The Bible verse often memorized by Sunday School kids around the world says;

For God so loved the world, that He gave His only begotten Son, that whoever believes in Him shall not perish, but have eternal life. For God did not send the Son into the world to judge the world, but that the world should be saved through Him.
(John 3:16-17)

I have no desire to bore you or confuse you with theological reasons why you should become a Follower of Jesus Christ. I definitely do desire that you have peace with God through a personal relationship with Him.
I know various ones say there are many ways to God, but the Bible says that, "*Jesus is the Way, the Truth, and the Life; no one comes to the Father but through Me*".
Seem narrow? Yeah. Is it true? Sure is. Cutting through all the smoke and mirrors Satan may throw at you, you simply humble yourself before God and ask Jesus to come into your life, to forgive your sins, and be the Lord of your life.
God loves you! Why don't you let Him carry things from here?

If you make this commitment to Jesus, you may wish to sign your name and the date as a reminder.

Lord Jesus, here's my commitment to you ----------

Name: _____ **Date** _____

Thank you for your extreme love, grace, and mercy!

May His blessing and favor be yours eternally!

Dave

ISBN 1-41206531-3